Anthropology

Teacher Edition

Written by Rebecca Stark

Cover Design by Susan Banta
Illustrations by Nelsy Fontalvo
and Karen Neulinger

**Educational
Impressions**

The purchase of this book entitles the buyer to exclusive
reproduction rights. Permission to reproduce these
pages is extended to the purchaser only.

Explanation of cover design: The dancers on the cover represent a rock
painting of the Bushmen, a nomadic people of southwestern Africa. Their
art is naturalistic and full of vitality.

ISBN: 0-56644-959-6

© 1986 Educational Impressions, Inc., Hawthorne, NJ
Revised 1993

EDUCATIONAL IMPRESSIONS, INC.
Hawthorne, NJ 07507

Table of Contents

To the Teacher

Anthropology is the scientific study of humankind. It is the objective of this book to introduce students to this fascinating subject and the subfields into which it is divided. Students learn about the beginnings of anthropology as an outgrowth of the curiosity stimulated by the Age of Exploration and how it grew into the basic field of study it is today. Major developments and theories of outstanding anthropologists are presented.

Students gain insight into the origins and evolution of the human species, as well as an understanding of the evolution of human culture. They become aware of the wide variety of recent and contemporary societies. As they learn about the differences among peoples' lifestyles and beliefs, however, they also learn that all peoples share certain basic needs. Perhaps most importantly, students come to realize that in spite of superficial differences, we are all members of a **single** human species!

The self-directed activities emphasize higher-level thinking skills and the activities have been keyed to Bloom's Taxonomy* for your convenience. Although not so marked, other higher-level skills such as fluency, flexibility, originality and risk-taking are also encouraged.

I hope you and your students enjoy learning about the most fascinating animal of all—the human species!

Bloom's Taxonomy

KNOWLEDGE (K): The recall of specifics and universals; bringing to mind the appropriate material.

COMPREHENSION (C): Understanding what is being communicated and making use of what is being communicated without necessarily relating it to other material or seeing its fullest implications.

APPLICATION (AP): The use of abstractions in particular and concrete situations. The abstractions may be in the form of general or technical ideas, rules or methods which must be remembered and applied.

ANALYSIS (AN): Breaking down a communication into its constituent elements or parts so that the relative hierarchy of ideas expressed are made explicit.

SYNTHESIS (S): Putting together elements and parts to form a whole; arranging and combining the elements in a pattern or structure not clearly there before.

EVALUATION (E): Making judgments about the extent to which material and methods satisfy criteria, either given to the student or determined by the student.

Benjamin Bloom. *Taxonomy of Educational Objectives. Handbook 1: Cognitive Domain.* New York: David McKay, 1956.

What Is Anthropology?

Anthropology is the study of human beings—both fossil and living—at all times and in all places. The term is based upon two Greek words: *anthropos,* meaning "man" and *logia* meaning "study." As humans are a part of nature, anthropology must be considered a natural science. Anthropologists must be careful that the data they collect is in accordance with scientific methods and principles. In other words, it must be verifiable.

But anthropology is not only a natural science, it is also a social science, for human beings are culture-producing animals. Culture is the system of learned behavior patterns, beliefs, arts and institutions characteristic of the society. Anthropologists study the various elements and systems within the society in order to attempt to comprehend the whole society. They believe that each element and system within a society is linked in some way to other elements within the society; therefore, the society cannot be accurately understood without an understanding of its parts and vice versa.

Every culture has certain needs which must be met. Because we are all members of a single species, many of the needs are the same for all cultures. In order to meet those universal needs, cultures all have certain basic systems: social organization, economic organization, political organization, technology, art and language. The anthropologist studies these various aspects of culture and tries to explain why variations occur. The primary goal of anthropology is to gain knowledge about the nature of human beings and their relationships to their natural and cultural environments; however, the knowledge gained can also help us cope with the problems facing human beings in today's world.

Branches of Anthropology

The interests of anthropology are exremely diversified; therefore, it is necessary for anthropologists to specialize. The two main subdivisions are physical, or biological, anthropology and cultural anthropology. Cultural anthropology, which deals with the learned behavior in human societies, is further divided into archaeology, ethnology and linguistics.

Physical anthropologists are primarily concerned with the biological, physical and genetic characteristics of human populations. They deal with our evolutionary origins and development and study how humans have adapted biologically to their environments.

Archaeology, the first major branch of **cultural anthropology,** focuses on the reconstruction of past cultures through the study of material evidence. The remains that archaeologists study include everything made by human beings—from the simplest tools to the most elaborate palaces. They call those objects made or produced by human workmanship *artifacts*.

The second, and possibly the most basic division of cultural anthropology, is **ethnology.** *Ethnos* means "race" and *logia* means "study." Ethnologists study and describe human societies; however, they do not stop there. They also study the origins of the cultures and attempt to learn how and why the cultures changed and developed as they did. In doing so, the ethnologist is necessarily concerned with interrelationships: between peoples and their environment, between different cultures, between different aspects of their culture, etc.

The third division, **linguistics,** is the science of language. Although it is considered by some to be a separate science, language is an aspect of culture. Linguistic anthropologists focus upon the sociocultural context of language. They study the patterns of language behavior of a large sample of peoples in an attempt to find universal attributes, or qualities, that would explain how languages change. They study the relations between a people's language and the other aspects of their culture.

1. What might an anthropologist do to be certain that his/her data is verifiable? (K, C, AN)

_____

_____

_____

2. Make a poster that illustrates the basic needs of all peoples. (K, C, AP)

3. Make a chart that shows the major subdivisions and fields of anthropology. (C, AN)

Developments in Anthropology

Although the explorers and conquistadores were not anthropologists, their journals and accounts of their voyages did provide opportunities for Europeans to study other cultures. Their works were more ethnographies, or descriptions, than ethnologies. They were not systematic enough to be thought of as anthropology.

In 1724 a Catholic missionary, Father François Lafitau, who worked among the Iroquois and Hurons of western New York, published a comparative ethnology. It was entitled "Customs of the American Savages, Compared with the Customs of Early Times." Although the principles he set forth are now taken for granted, he was one of the first to clarify them: 1) contemporary and ancient cultures throw light on one another; 2) historic relations between cultures can only be determined if careful analysis shows that specific traits are significantly similar; and 3) that we must evaluate other cultures in terms of **their** standards and not our own.

Charles Darwin

Even before 1859 when Charles Darwin published his monumental book, *Origin of Species,* there had been a growth in the interest in and study of the origin of the human species. By the middle of the nineteenth century it had become easier to discuss this and other controversial issues such as the following: Is there only one human species? Did the human species change? Although Darwin was not the first to advocate the principle of evolution, he was the first to provide substantial evidence and to clearly explain the principle. What's more, his work firmly established the human species as a subject within the realm of the natural sciences.

4. Darwin proposed that man successfully evolved and adapted because of his powerful brain. Use Darwin's theory of natural selection to explain what he meant. (C, AP)

_____

_____

_____

_____

_____

Linear Evolutionism

Along with the idea of human evolution went the theory of cultural evolution. Lewis Henry Morgan, an American anthropologist, the Scottish John F. MacLennan and Englishman Edward B. Tylor were the principal proponents of cultural evolution. Known as the linear interpretation of history, the theory they advocated proposed that societies pass through several stages from the simple to the complex. They believed that *human nature* was similar among all people; therefore, the order, although not necessarily the speed, was inevitable. Edward Tylor stressed that the reason some societies could skip certain stages in development was due to diffusion, or the borrowing of knowledge from other cultures.

5. Research and chart the stages of cultural evolution according to Morgan's theory. (C, AP)

The Evolution of Religion

Morgan did not feel that an evolutionary sequence could be established for religious forms; nevertheless, in 1874 his British contemporary Edward Tylor published his great work which dealt primarily with the evolutionary development of religion in culture. It was entitled *Primitive Culture: Researches into the Development of Mythology, Philosophy, Religion, Language, Art and Custom.* In 1890 Sir James Frazer published *Golden Bough,* in which he proposed that early peoples invented magic in an attempt to control natural forces and that they turned to religion when magic failed to do its job. Although *Golden Bough* has many flaws in its method and theory, it is a fascinating collection of ethnographies.

6. Draw a picture that illustrates Tylor's theory of how animism evolved. (C, AP)

Franz Boas and Historical Reconstruction

In the twentieth century, research became more methodical and less speculative. One of the first to react against speculation and to stress the importance of fieldwork and first-hand observation was Franz Boas, a German-born American. Although he was not the first to hold such a view, Boas also believed it was valuable to record the statements made by informants in their own language. The main reason Boas and his followers reacted against the methodology of the cultural evolutionists was that they often selected facts to further their theories and that they examined isolated traits without regard to the culture as a whole. Boas believed that all elements of a culture interrelate to make up a functioning whole.

7. Boas had a great influence upon a number of distinguished anthropologists. He inspired them to go the field to gather facts and to make detailed, objective recordings of what they observed. Among his students were the following men and women: Ruth Benedict, Alfred L. Kroeber, Margaret Mead and Edward Sapir. Research these people and summarize their contributions to anthropology. Choose one of them and design an award in honor of his/her achievements. (C, AP, AN, S, E)

Functionalism and Structuralism

Some anthropologists reacted against cultural evolutionism by rejecting the relevance of cultural history altogether. They stressed the importance of studying living societies.

Bronislaw Malinowski (1884-1942) and his followers insisted that comparison of cultures was a waste of time. They felt the only thing that matters is how an element functions in the present culture. Furthermore, they proposed that every custom, attitude and act has a function and that nothing should be overlooked. A.R. Radcliffe-Brown (1888-1955) and others moved on from functionalism to a concern with social structure. They stressed that because all aspects of a culture are interrelated, that change in one aspect will cause a change in another aspect of the culture. A culture trait may have more than one function in relation to a system of which it is a part. It may have a positive, or beneficial (eufunctional), effect on some aspects of culture and a negative, or harmful (dysfunctional) effect on other aspects. It may have another effect that is neither positive nor negative. The functions themselves may be manifest, or obvious and intended, or they may be latent, or unintended and often unperceived.

8. Cite an example of an aspect of a culture that has both a positive and a negative function and explain. (C, AP)

_____

_____

_____

_____

Human Evolution

The Roots of Humanity

Scientists believe that man's ancestors first lived about 70 million years ago in the form of small, four-footed, tree-dwelling animals much like the tree shrews of today. As primates—members of the order to which humans belong—grew larger, they began to grasp tree trunks with the fore and hind limbs.

Australopithecine

The next stage was brachiation, or arm swinging. This stage lasted a long time for apes. Evidence of this is in their long arms and the inefficiency of their legs in walking. The direct ancestors of man, however, evolved from this stage in a relatively short time. They took to the ground. These humanlike primates were the australopithecines.

1. Make a chart or poster that shows the main characteristics of a primate. (C, AP)

2. Opposability of the thumb (freedom to move the thumb in a swinging action across the palm of the hand) made a gradual appearance through primate evolution. It is fully developed only in humans. First predict what would happen if you didn't have use of your thumbs. Then tape your thumbs to your palms. What activities were inhibited by the loss of your thumbs? Record the results of the experiment. How did the results differ from your predictions? (AP, AN)

_____

_____

_____

_____

_____

3. Humans have evolved quickly because of their adaptability. Perhaps the most important change, in addition to increased brain power, was the freeing of the hands from their function of locomotion. Analyze the importance of this change. (C, AN)

_____

_____

_____

_____

_____

4. Draw a series of three pictures to show how our hands have evolved. (A, AP)

Gibbon	Chimpanzee (Ape)	Homo (Human)

5. Many of our generalizations about chimpanzees are based upon the studies done by Jane Goodall and her associates of one troop of chimpanzees along the shores of Lake Tanganyka. Evaluate the fact that many scientists use Goodall's findings to generalize about all wild chimpanzees. (AN, E)

_____

_____

_____

_____

Australopithecines

The australopithecines of south and east Africa were the first upright, bipedal hominid (belonging to the order Hominidae, of which *Homo sapiens* are the only extant members), fossil primates. Some of their features were still ape-like: small brain, massive projecting jaws and large molar teeth. Many of their features, however, were humanlike: smooth, rounded heads of the juveniles; teeth in a semicircular arch; the manner in which they chewed; delicate arms; and a vertical stance and gait which freed their hands for manipulation. Although these creatures were small and did not have any special weapons, such as horns or tusks, they used their superior intelligence to compete for survival.

6. Olduvai Gorge in east Africa has been called the "Grand Canyon of Human Evolution." Research the finds which have been made there and evaluate its nickname. (C, E)

_____

_____

_____

7. Circle the word on this page meaning "still in existence." (K)

Homo Erectus (Pithecanthropines)

As human evolution continued, the new hominids—collectively known as pithecanthropines—appeared: Java Man, Peking Man, Heidelberg Man and others. They are included in the species *Homo erectus* and were characterized by increased brain size and mental powers. Like the australopithecines, members of the *Homo erectus* species were also hunters and makers of specialized tools; however, Peking Man added the controlled use of fire. The site at Torralba, Spain, for example, shows that fire was used in animal drives and for cooking.

8. Evaluate the importance of the mastery of fire. (C, AN, E)

_____

_____

_____

Homo Sapiens

Evolution continued and in the Middle Paleolithic Period *Homo sapiens* appeared. *Sapiens* is the Latin word for "intelligent." Hunting and gathering continued to be the source of sustenance, but the techniques were changing. Hand axes were refined and flake tools were gaining in importance. One important development was in shelter. Although many still lived in caves, others built houses large enough to hold a small band. The band was probably the basic unit of social life.

A specialized variation of *Homo sapiens* was *Homo sapiens neandertalensis*. In 1856 a skull and bones were found by workers who were blasting in a limestone cave near Dusseldorf, Germany. They were the remains of Neanderthal Man. At first scientists described Neanderthal Man as "brutish," "of a savage race" and "idiotic." Later finds show that those scientists had been too quick to make their judgments. The Neanderthalers seem to have led a complex and sensitive life. Their short, stocky build was probably an adaptation to harsh conditions of the Ice Age.

9. The discovery at the cave near Dusseldorf was an accidental find. In what other occupations might accidental finds of fossil remains or artifacts be likely? (C)

_____

_____

_____

10. The Neanderthalers are associated with the Mousterian tool complex. Research and report on the characteristics of the Mousterian tool industry. (C, AP)

_____

_____

_____

_____

_____

Modern Humans

Modern humans—*Homo sapiens sapiens*—emerged during the third interglacial period. Many scientists believe that the species directly descended from the Neanderthals; some disagree. In either case, it is clear that it evolved from the same genetic pool. By the middle of the fourth glacial period, Neanderthal populations had disappeared and modern man had taken over. From that time on there has been one—and only one—genus, species and subspecies of human beings: *Homo sapiens sapiens*. Although there have been no drastic physical changes in the evolution of human beings in the period that followed, there have been great evolutionary changes in human culture!

11. Make a time line that shows the major types of hominids: *Australopithecus, Homo erectus,* and *Homo sapiens.* Also show the glacial and interglacial periods. (C, AP)

12. Cro-Magnon people are probably the best known, although not the only, variety of Upper Paleolithic *Homo sapiens sapiens.* European and American authors have written much about them. Research the Cro-Magnons and speculate as to why Europeans and Americans believed for so long that they were our only true ancestors. (K, C, AN)

13. L.S.B. Leakey (1903-1972) was a noted archaeologist and anthropologist. Research his work and design a postage stamp in his honor. It should illustrate his greatest contribution to our knowledge of human evolution (C, AN, S, E)

The Ages of Man

The Ages of Man are based upon the tools that were made.

Prehistoric Man

From the very beginning human beings made things. At first they probably used soft materials, such as wood or bone, that bent easily. Then they learned to fashion tools from flint (a fine-grained quartz) by chipping off the edges. As time went on they learned to use other materials. Because so much of what they learned about prehistoric times came from the stone artifacts they found, archaeologists called this period of time the Stone Age. Scholars later divided it into two distinct periods: the Paleolithic (Old Stone) Age and the Neolithic (New Stone) Age. Some of the most fantastic discoveries of the Stone Age were made by English anthropologist L.S.B. Leakey. Among his finds were the stone tools and skeletal remains of early man which date back two million years. They were found in Tanzania.

Paleolithic (Old Stone) Age: During this age people were merely food finders. They had crude stone tools with which to hunt or gather their food and to protect themselves.

Neolithic (New Stone) Age: During this age people began to produce food. They discovered farming and learned to tame animals. Polished stone tools were made in this period.

Civilization

Civilization was born in the Near East about 5,000 years ago with the rise of Sumer in the Valley of the Tigris and Euphrates Rivers and slightly later in Egypt. In most places civilization was accompanied by two inventions: writing and metallurgy (the process of removing metal from ore). Metallurgy, of course, led to the making of metal tools. The ages of man in these stages, too, are classified according to the tools that were made. At first tools were made out of copper, but pure copper is too soft to be effective. Eventually, people learned to harden the copper with alloys.

Bronze Age: The true formula for bronze, 90% copper and 10% tin, was first discovered late in the third millennium B.C.

Iron Age: The art of smelting iron seems to have been discovered *c.* 1200 B.C. in the Taurus Mountains of Asia Minor.

1. In what age do we live? (K) _____

2. Archaeologists use these ages to classify settlements. Explain why it is not possible to use these ages as a guide to exact dates. (C)

_____

_____

Human Variation

Since the middle of the Upper Pleistocene Epoch every living man, woman and child has belonged to the same genus, species and subspecies: *Homo sapiens sapiens.*

1. A species is said to be a closed genetic system and a subspecies is said to be an open system. Explain what is meant by these terms. (C, AP)

_____

_____

_____

_____

2. Use the fact that there is only one human species as the basis for an anti-segregation/anti-apartheid speech. (C, AP, AN, S)

Natural Selection

Gene pools may be altered in a variety of ways; one of the most important is natural selection. Natural selection is based on the principle that forms which are better adapted to their environment will live longer and will produce more offspring; therefore, in that environment the population with the adaptation will grow.

3. Use natural selection to give a possible explanation for variations among humans in pigmentation of skin and hair. (K, C, AP, AN)

_____

_____

_____

_____

4. How do Eskimos exemplify adaptation to cold climate? (C, AP, AN)

_____

_____

_____

_____

_____

Scottish historian William Robertson made this statement in 1777: "At his first appearance in the state of infancy, whether it be among the rudest savages or in the most civilized nations, we can discern no quality which marks any distinction or superiority. The capacity for improvement seems to be the same and the talents he may afterwards acquire....The virtues he may be rendered capable of exercising, depend in great measure upon the state of society in which he is placed."

5. Predict what might have happened if an Iroquois baby had been adopted at birth by a Pueblo family. Describe his/her world view as an adult. (C, AN)

_____

_____

_____

_____

6. Write a story about identical twins who were separated at birth and brought up in totally different environments. In what ways might their lives be influenced by heredity? In what ways might their lives be influenced by their environments? (AN, S, E)

Culture and Society

Culture is the total integrated system of socially transmitted behavior patterns, arts, beliefs, institutions, workmanship and thoughts that are shared by the members of a society. These products and behaviors are governed by a set of rules which are accepted by those members.

The way in which the aspects of culture are patterned is unique for that society. But cultures are not stable; they change. Changes occur as a result of intergroup contact and inventions as well as environmental conditions. Perhaps the most important fact about human culture is that it is passed on from generation to generation. Humans are unique in that they **learn** a much greater proportion of their behavior patterns than any other animal. Every human society has its own distinct culture, and members of each society acquire their culture from other members of the same society.

1. Predict what would happen if ten babies were raised from birth without any other human contact. Somehow their dietary needs are met. They will be a society, but will they create culture? (C, AN)

_____

_____

_____

_____

_____

2. Find out what is meant by culture shock. Write a short story in which the main character or characters experience such a phenomenon. Be sure to describe the feelings and reactions of your character(s). (C, AN, S, E)

3. Society and culture are not synonyms. Societies are people. Just as people have needs, so do the societies of which they are a part. Write an analogy that expresses the relationship of society to culture. (C, AP, AN)

_____ : _____ : : _____ : _____

4. The culture of a society must meet the society's needs if the society is to survive. Create a poster that illustrates what these needs are and how they are met by the culture of the society of which you are a member. (C, AP, AN, E)

Subsistence Techniques

The Search for Food

Although all people must obtain food, what they obtain and how they obtain it differ. These things depend upon the natural environment, the size of the population and the culture of the society.

There are four basic levels of subsistence, or means of maintaining life:

Hunting and Gathering
Intensive Foraging
Incipient Agriculture (Horticulture) and Pastoralism
Intensive Agriculture (Plow Culture)

1. Although there may be overlapping, the above levels of subsistence fall into two general categories: gathering and production. Explain the main differences between the two. (C)

_____

_____

_____

2. With each higher level, the production techniques lower the amount of energy expended. Analyze the effect upon other aspects of a society's culture. (C, AN)

_____

_____

_____

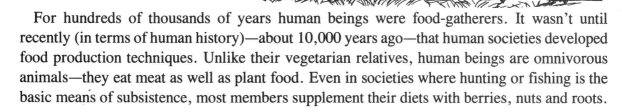

Hunting and Gathering

For hundreds of thousands of years human beings were food-gatherers. It wasn't until recently (in terms of human history)—about 10,000 years ago—that human societies developed food production techniques. Unlike their vegetarian relatives, human beings are omnivorous animals—they eat meat as well as plant food. Even in societies where hunting or fishing is the basic means of subsistence, most members supplement their diets with berries, nuts and roots.

3. Although food-gathering societies may differ from each other in many other ways, they tend to have certain things in common. Make a chart showing the general characteristics of food-gatherers. (C, AP)

4. Create a poster entitled "Paleolithic Weapons." (C, AP)

The Eskimo Whale Hunt

In many societies, hunting involves more than tracking and killing. The Eskimo Whale Hunt, for example, also involves an intricate network of beliefs and behaviors which manifest themselves in the Whale Cult.

Membership in the Whale Cult is extremely limited. It is obtained only after intense instruction in which the apprentices must learn the proper rituals and songs and seek a vision. The songs are private property and are passed on from father to son. So are the special amulets, or charms, which are worn to ward off evil and injury.

The hunting season is marked by ceremonies and taboos. The whalers are kept apart from the other villagers; their activities and food are strictly limited. The tools and weapons to be used by the whalers are thoroughly cleaned and repaired so as not to offend the whale. The boats are prepared in ceremonies which often include the presence of deceased whalers.

Once the kill has been made, the whale is brought ashore. The chief's wife gives it a symbolic drink and it is also given food. Other ceremonies are solemnly performed to ensure that the whale's spirit will return to the sea unangered. The rituals last for three to five days.

Social and economic leadership is closely tied to leadership of the hunt. The headman of the whaling crew is also the leader of the local group. Distribution of the whale parts is governed by custom. The boat owner, harpooners and others important to the hunt are given special rights.

5. Analyze the use of magic and ritual in the Whale Hunt. (C, AN, E)

_____

_____

_____

Intensive Foraging

Although intensive foragers and hunter-gatherers both rely on a mixed meat and vegetarian diet, the two groups differ in their emphasis. Whereas the hunter-gatherer has a basic diet of meat and supplements it with wild plants, the intensive forager's diet comprises mostly wild plant life and is supplemented by meat. Bands of foragers are usually semi-nomadic and tend to stay within the territory that is familiar to them. Although they do not accumulate much property, they do have some tools and weapons.

6. The Shoshone were nineteenth-century Desert Culture foragers. Each band specialized in the collection of a specific food and was so named: Seed Eaters, Pine Nut Eaters, and so on. Plan a buffet dinner that would include some favorite foods of the Shoshone. (C, AP)

Incipient Agriculture (Horticulture) and Pastoralism

The domestication of plants and animals evolved at different times in different parts of the world. Domestication spread during the Neolithic, or New Stone, Age.

Horticulture

A domesticated plant is one that is useful and whose cultivation and breeding is controlled. The domestication of plants probably occurred gradually. Perhaps gatherers noticed that where dried seeds had fallen into moist earth, new grasses grew. Some may have observed that stalks of edible plants sprouted new shoots when put back into the earth. The first type of cultivation probably involved weed control. They might have noticed that weeds, or undesirable plants, grew back after they had cleared them from an area of wild plants they had been tending. When seeds, roots or shoots were intentionally planted and stored for future use, real domestication began.

There seem to be four major crop complexes of primitive agriculture. Two of them are adapted to dry uplands and seasonal variations in climate: the dry-rice cultivation of central Borneo (Old World) and maize cultivation by the Maya (New World). The other two complexes are adapted to tropical rain forests: yam cultivation in Africa, Melanesia and New Guinea and wet-rice cultivation in the Orient (Old World) and manioc, or cassava, cultivation in South America (New World). We use the term horticulture to describe this type of gardening which involves cultivation of domestic plants without the use of a plow.

7. Horticulture, or gardening, does not include the use of a plow, but it does make use of other tools. Create a poster that illustrates the tools of the horticulturist. (C, AP)

8. In forested areas, horticulture first requires clearing the forest for planting. Draw a diagram that explains the slash-and-burn method. (C, AP)

9. The domestication of plants brought about the first major socio-cultural revolution in human history. Analyze the social and cultural changes that this technological innovation precipitated. (C, AN)

_____

_____

_____

_____

Pastoralism

In regions where the environment was not suited to the raising of crops, people developed a subsistence technique which centered around the herding, breeding and raising of livestock, known as pastoralism. Like horticulture, pastoralism spread during the Neolithic Age.

Among the earliest animals to be domesticated were dogs and goats, followed by sheep, cattle and pigs. Pastoral people are usually semi-nomadic. They move according to the needs of the animals; however, they tend to remain within certain limits and to return to the same locations each season.

10. Pastoralists are not the only ones to have domesticated animals. Make a bulletin board display that shows at least six practical uses of domesticated animals. (C, AP)

11. The relationship between a herdsman and his animals is symbiotic. Create a poster or a cartoon that shows the ways in which the animals might benefit from the association. (AN)

Intensive Agriculture (Plow Culture)

The invention of the plow was one of the most important developments in human history. It was probably invented in the Middle East. At first the plow was likely a device to pull a wooden hoe through the ground by manpower; it wasn't until later that oxen were trained for that purpose. In any event, once adapted, its use spread rapidly.

The effects of plow cultivation were tremendous. Large areas could be prepared for sowing in a short period of time. Less energy was needed and, therefore, the productivity of the laborer increased. Areas previously too difficult to work could now be cultivated. With this new agriculture, populations grew. Land shortages resulted and people had to search for new lands. This, in turn, led to the diffusion, or spread, of the plow to those areas at a phenomenally rapid rate.

Although the plow and the use of draft animals were important, they were not the only innovations which led to the development of true agriculture. True agriculture also involves other ways of increasing productivity: selective breeding of the animals, seed selection, fertilization, and perhaps most importantly, irrigation. Irrigation-based agriculture became especially important in areas which get little rainfall (the Middle East, for example). With the discovery of irrigation, people could extend their farmlands and cultivate them during periods previously too dry. Extensive waterworks were established in the Tigris-Euphrates Valley of Mesopotamia, along the banks of the Lower Nile, over the alluvial plain of the Indus, in the Huang Ho Valley of China, along the coast of Peru and in the Mexican basin.

12. Analyze the reasons that the irrigation-based agriculture was closely related to the emergence of other cultural institutions. (AN)

_____

_____

_____

Early Civilization: The Urban Revolution

With the great technological advancements in gardening which developed in the Neolithic Age in the great river valleys of the Euphrates and Tigris in Mesopotamia, the Nile in Egypt and the Indus in western Pakistan, came what might be called the Urban Revolution. Towns developed into cities, and "civilization" was born.

V.G. Childe listed in *The Urban Revolution* (1950) ten characteristics of early civilization:

Ten Characteristics of Early Civilization as Noted by Childe

1. There is an enlarged organized society and, therefore, a wider level of social integration.

2. The surpluses of farmers and artisans are centrally accumulated.

3. Workers specialize and systems of redistribution and exchange of goods are devised.

4. Specialization and exchange are expanded and far-reaching trade is established.

5. Monumental public works are constructed and maintained through central organization of available time; this is made possible because that time is no longer needed for food production or basic manufacturing.

6. Art forms express symbolic identification and provide aesthetic enjoyment.

7. The art of writing is developed.

8. Arithmetic, geometry and astronomy are developed.

9. A well-structured political organization in which membership is based upon residence replaces the one in which membership is based upon kinship.

10. A privileged ruling class of religious, political and military functionaries organizes and directs the system.

---

1. Choose an ancient civilization. Write a report that details how it exemplifies the ten characteristics of early civilization as noted by Childe. (C, AP, AN)

Technological Adaptations

The most fundamental cultural products and techniques are those related to the quest for and production of food. Others, although not as vital as those related to food, are shelter, clothing and transport. These and other technological adaptations have made it possible for humans to survive in all types of environments.

Shelter

There are a number of factors upon which the technological adaptations of a culture depend. Some basic factors in nonliterate societies are climate, the kinds of building materials available and whether or not their quest for food requires movement from one place to another. The societies dependent upon agriculture for subsistence tend to be the most sedentary; therefore, they usually build more elaborate dwellings in which they plan to live for long periods of time. Foragers, on the other hand, tend to build simple shelters, expending the least amount of energy possible. Another factor affecting housing adaptation is the extent of their transport techniques. The Plains Indians, for example, were hunters who moved seasonally. Because they had dogs and horses, they were able to make use of the portable tent.

Anthropologists identify five types of settlement patterns. A settlement pattern is the spatial arrangement of a society's subgroups. The basic patterns are migratory, or nomadic bands; scattered neighborhoods; semi-nomadic (or semi-sedentary) communities; compact, permanent towns or villages and complex towns with outlying settlements; and compact, impermanent villages shifting locations every few years. Many factors affect the internal arrangements of settlements. Especially important are factors of social organization such as kinship groupings and class, caste and sexual stratification.

1. Make a collage of the types of shelter around the world. (AP)

2. Prepare a how-to booklet on how to build an igloo. (K, C, AP)

3. Evaluate the efficiency of the tipi of the Plains Indians. (C, AN, E)

_____

_____

_____

_____

4. Make a cut-away drawing of an Iroquois longhouse. (C, AP)

5. Make a diorama of a Pueblo village. Analyze the relation of their communal houses to their culture. (C, AP, AN, E)

Clothing and Ornaments

Although an important function of clothing is to protect against the weather and other elements of the environment, it is seldom the only function. Most clothing also serves as adornment; in almost all cultures people clothe and decorate themselves in a manner believed to improve their appearance. In most societies clothing also serves as a means of covering those parts of the body considered improper or immodest to reveal. What is considered improper varies greatly among societies. Clothing functions in another important way: it reflects the social, political, economic or occupational status of its wearer.

1. What is considered proper or indecent varies greatly from one society to the next. It may also vary from one situation to the next within the society. Create a cartoon based upon your own culture to illustrate a situation in which clothing is not appropriate to the occasion. (C, AP, S)

2. Except in the coldest regions of the world, most headgear has little to do with climate. Make a poster illustrating a variety of head coverings. Classify your examples according to their functions. (C, AP, AN)

3. Draw a series of pictures to show how hairstyles may symbolize social position. (C, AP, AN)

4. Tatooing is a form of ornamentation practiced in several societies; however, it is not associated with the same statuses in all societies. Use the status associations of tatooing in Polynesia and in America to illustrate this point. (C, AP)

_____

_____

_____

_____

Transport

As technology advanced in other areas, so did systems of transport. Hunter-gatherers had to carry all of their goods with them. Human energy provided for most of their transport needs. They were aided by pathways, footwear and containers. When people learned to use animals to transport their burdens, efficiency increased. The relatively recent invention of the wheel improved efficiency of land transportation even more.

Means of water transport probably developed earlier and at a quicker rate than land transport. People noticed how objects floated down a river or stream. Sooner or later some got the idea to copy the phenomenon. The earlist forms of water transport were, therefore, rafts and floats. True boats came later.

As transportation developed, trade between different cultures was stimulated. It became more and more difficult for a society to remain isolated. Today modern transportation makes us more and more a "world community."

1. Make a bulletin board display of early means of land and water transport. (C, AP)

2. Make a model travois. (C, AP)

3. Design a postage stamp to commemorate the most important advance in land transportation. (C, AN, E)

4. Judge the importance of the development of ocean travel upon the history of culture. (C, AN, E)

_____

_____

_____

Tools and Handicrafts

All peoples make tools and containers in order to meet their other material needs: food, shelter, clothing and transport. In general, foragers make the simplest tools and containers. They use materials which are readily available and which require as little processing as possible. The most basic tools are those used for cutting, such as knives, choppers, chisels, scrapers and borers. Early cutting tools were made by chipping or polishing stone in a number of ways. The earliest containers were also made of readily available materials.

Some foragers make woven baskets, but few make pottery or have knowledge of metallurgy, the science of mining, smelting ore and working the metal into useful objects. With the development of primitive farming and then agriculture, the tools and containers became more complex. As the subsistence methods became more efficient, there were greater surpluses of food. This led to the need for storage containers, cooking equipment and transport for trading.

1. Make a counter top display of materials used by foragers to make tools, weapons and containers. (K, AP)

2. We call the Paleolithic and Neolithic Periods the Stone Age because of the tools that were made; however, there were probably tools and containers of other materials as well. Why don't we usually mention those other materials? (C, AN)

_____

_____

_____

3. Research two Native American groups. Compare and contrast their tools, weapons and containers. (C, AN)

4. Make a flipbook of utensils and other artifacts which could be made out of a simple shell. Stretch your imagination and include some unusual ideas! (C, AP, S)

Baskets were among the earliest containers and most people of the world possess some knowledge of basketry techniques. Three basic techniques are coiling, weaving and twining.

5. The Pomo of California are renowned for their fine basketry. Make a bulletin board display illustrating the basketry of these people. Analyze why it is considered both a fine and a practical art. (C, AP, AN)

_____

_____

_____

_____

6. Draw diagrams to illustrate the techniques of weaving, coiling and twining. On the lines below, write a brief explanation of each. (C, AP)

Weaving	Coiling	Twining
_____	_____	_____
_____	_____	_____
_____	_____	_____
_____	_____	_____
_____	_____	_____
_____	_____	_____
_____	_____	_____

Basketry is suited to nomadic food gatherers because of its flexibility, strength and light weight. For the same reasons, hides are also important as material for containers among peoples whose subsistence techniques depend on travel.

8. Parfleches are the traveling bags of the Plains Indians. Made a parfleche. If rawhide is not available, use as heavy a material as possible. Decorate it with a geometric design. (C, AP, S)

Pottery was invented in the Mesolithic Period. In general, food gatherers and hunters do not bother with it. The making of pottery requires a detailed knowledge of the suitable materials, the processes of mixing the materials and the methods of shaping, drying, finishing and firing the vessels.

8. Why is pottery better suited to sedentary farmers than to nomadic foragers or hunters? (C, AN)

_____

_____

_____

_____

9. Archaeologists have learned a lot about the lifestyles and beliefs of ancient peoples from their pottery, for it was often decorated with everyday occurrences. Many peoples decorate their pottery with representations of their gods, goddesses and religious symbols. With this in mind, analyze the following statement: Because pottery was of so little value to the ancients, it is of great value to the archaeologists. (AN, EV)

_____

_____

_____

_____

Metalworking, like pottery-making, requires detailed knowledge of raw materials and the techniques of obtaining those materials and working them into finished products.

10. Chart the four main phases of working metal. (K, C, AP)

_____

_____

_____

_____

Economic Organization

For a society to survive, there must be some type of economic organization. In other words, there must be a network of rules governing the production, allocation, distribution, use and consumption of goods. Simple economic systems are those in which most of the food and goods is consumed by the producer and the members of the producer's immediate family or household. This type of consumption in which no exchange outside the primary family is necessary is called "primary" consumption. When exchange of food and goods outside the primary group of the original producer is involved, "secondary" consumption occurs.

1. In complex urban societies, primary consumption is extremely low. Think about all of the food, clothing, shelter and other goods you have used in the past few days. Did you or your immediate family produce any of them? (C)

_____

_____

_____

Property may take may forms: it may be personal property (individually owned); it may be joint property (group owned); or may be communal property (society owned). The property may be in the form of real estate or it may be movable. It may be material and concrete or it may be nonmaterial, such as songs, dances and names. In any case, the existence of the object itself does not constitute property. An object is not property unless the members of the society agree to recognize the limiting rights of use and disposition of an object. In almost all cases (even if an owner is said to have exclusive right of use), the rights of use are limited by the demands of society.

Land is a very important kind of property and is usually communal property. Hunting and gathering peoples need a flexible system for allocating access to natural resources in order to adjust to shifts in availability of food. Pastoral people tend not to establish property claims on land, but rather to treat the grazing resources as public domain. Agricultural people, on the other hand, tend to have a more developed concept of land ownership, for their subsistence is closely dependent upon the soil.

2. Analyze the following statement: "Land is the most important kind of property." Tell if you agree or disagree. (C, AN, E)

_____

_____

_____

_____

3. In order for a society to continue, there must be an orderly flow of property from one generation to the next. In societies based upon agriculture, where there is a growing population, there may be a problem of too many heirs for too limited an amount of land. Primogeniture is sometimes the solution. Find out what primogeniture is and evaluate its usefulness and fairness. (C, AN, E)

_____

_____

_____

_____

4. Pastoral peoples are often in conflict with farming peoples. Analyze the reasons for this conflict. (C, AN)

_____

_____

_____

_____

Modes of Exchange

There are three basic modes of exchange: reciprocity, redistribution and market exchange. **Reciprocity** is common in simple subsistence economies. It involves the equal giving and receiving of goods and services between persons of specific statuses within the social system. With systems based upon **redistribution,** the goods and services are moved toward an allocative center. A political or economic official has the power to distribute (or withhold) the goods or services. The redistribution may or may not be fair. Redistribution is more common in social systems with some social stratification. It is characteristic of several state-organized, nonliterate, horticultural societies and early civilizations, such as the Sumerian and the Mayan civilizations.

Market exchange came into existence as food-growing technologies became more productive. The surplus goods could be exchanged for other foods. Also, some people could be freed from food production in order to specialize in crafts and services. Early forms of market exchange were based upon the principle of barter. Barter is the direct exchange of one product or service for another through bargaining. Eventually, as specialization increased and became more complex, there grew a need for a medium of exchange that could be applied to all goods and services—money.

5. Barter is the practice of trading goods or services. Think of all of your needs. For one day try to acquire your needs by bartering with your friends. Do any problems arise? Report on the results of this experiment. (C, AP)

6. Sometimes trade among nonliterate people involves media of exchange other than money. Research the uses of wampum as a medium of exchange by Native Americans. How did its use change with the arrival of the Europeans. (C, AP)

_____

_____

_____

_____

_____

7. Fill in the appropriate mode of exchange for each described relationship. (C)

Transactional Mode

Underlying Social Relationship Expressed by the Transaction	Friendship, Kinship, Status Hierarchy	Political or Religious Affiliation	None

The Kula Ring of the Trobriand Islanders*

The Trobriand Islanders of southeast Melanesia are expert horticulturists and fishermen and usually produce more food than they can consume. Furthermore, portions of the labor force are employed in specialties not directly related to food production. Many of the specialized occupations, whether they relate to food production or manufacturing, are localized. The raw materials and technological specialization results in a surplus of some goods and a scarcity of others.

The Trobriand Islanders engage in a fascinating intertribal and interisland exchange system known as the Kula. It is based upon the greatly ritualized reciprocal exchange of nonutilitarian, but highly valued, goods: white shell armbands and long, red spondylus-shell necklaces. The armbands, called *mwali,* are always traded in a counterclockwise direction. The necklaces, called *soulava,* are always traded in a clockwise direction. There are no exceptions.

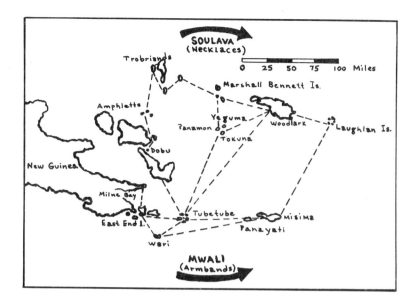

A limited number of men from each island take part in the Kula. Each has permanent lifelong partners with whom to trade. Each man receives the article, keeps it for a while and then passes it on. When he passes it on, he receives the opposite article in exchange. The transactions are strictly regulated by traditional rules and are accompanied by rituals and formalities to solidify the relationships. Each partner serves as the other's host and protector during these visits.

Associated with the Kula are important secondary activities. The ceremonial exchange of objects between partners is followed by trade of a more practical nature. When a member of the ring leaves to visit his partners, he brings with him locally grown and produced goods with which to trade. He trades them for goods grown and produced in his partners' islands but not available in his own. The types of commodities traded are foods such as bananas, coconuts and garden crops as well as artifacts made by the local craftsmen.

*This description is based upon the account of noted British archaeologist Bronislaw Malinowski.

8. Evaluate the benefits of the Kula to the trading partners. (AN, E)

_____

_____

_____

_____

_____

_____

_____

Social Organization

Human beings are social animals. Because of their reliance on one another, they organize themselves into groups. The patterned ways in which these groups and individuals are organized and their relationships to one another is that society's social structure, or social organization. The most important group for human beings is the family; however, most people also organize themselves into other groups that complement, extend and/or replace the family. In any society there are tasks to be done and people who are expected to do them. Every society classifies its members into a system of statuses; for example, age, sex, marital condition and kinship relations. Each status is associated with a set of behavior patterns; this characteristic and expected social behavior of an individual is his or her role.

In societies that are technologically less developed, such as hunter-gatherers and primitive farmers, there is usually no real social stratification. The groups that are differentiated on the basis of their roles in production are more or less equal. The little status differentiation that exists is usually confined to individuals or perhaps a few kin groups. In these societies, where some degree of social superiority is recognized, it usually takes the form of ranking, or assigning each status a position in a graded hierarchy.

As technology advances, more efficient production techniques lead to a greater surplus of subsistence goods. This in turn leads to greater specialization and diversification. As the need for systematic organization increases, some people gain control of the society's technology and economic system. Those who own or have the right to regulate productive goods—land, waterworks, industry, etc.—gain a great deal of power. These differences in the relationships of people to the technology and economic system usually result in social stratification. Social stratification means that some groups of people are recognized by themselves and others as having more or less right to certain things than do members of other groups of people in the same society. Those things include not only material goods, but also power, prestige, offices, jobs, leadership roles, etc. Social stratification is closely tied to the basic values of a society.

1. Everyone has many statuses and, therefore, manifests many roles. For example, a person behaves differently at home and at work. Make a chart of your many statuses. Describe the roles, or expected behavior, you manifest for each. (C, AN)

2. Analyze the universal human need to belong to some kind of group, usually based initially on family ties. (C, AN)

_____

_____

_____

_____

3. Compare and contrast ascribed and achieved statuses. Give examples of at least five statuses you have achieved and five which were ascribed to you. (C, AN)

_____

_____

_____

_____

_____

Achieved Statuses   **Ascribed Statuses**

1.   1.

2.   2.

3.   3.

4.   4.

5.   5.

4. Every society assigns different roles to men and women, with the females often being the subordinate group. In recent years, however—especially in some of the highly industrialized societies—women have reacted against this system of sexual stratification. What changes do you notice within your own community that reflect the rise in women's status? (C, AN)

_____

_____

_____

_____

_____

5. In most societies elderly people are respected; however, they are valued more in some societies than in others. Analyze the fact that old people seem to more highly venerated, or regarded with respect, in stable societies than in rapidly changing societies. (AN)

_____

_____

_____

Transition Rites

As a person moves through the developmental stages of the life cycle—birth, maturity, reproduction and death—he or she changes statuses. The transition is often a difficult period of time, for the person must leave familiar roles and has not yet acquired the new roles associated with the new status. These changes in status are often perceived as crises.

6. In order to help members handle these life crises, or transitional phases, most societies mark these phases by transition rites. Make a chronological chart of the transition rites you have gone through and will go through during your life cycle. (C, AP)

7. All human societies practice naming. Most ceremonially name and present their infants as new members of the society. As a person's life progresses, his or ner names often change. Sometimes new names are added to indicate a change in status. Keeping this in mind, evaluate the statement made by Juliet in William Shakespeare's *Romeo and Juliet:* ''What's in a name? That which we call a rose by any other name would smell as sweet.'' (AN)

_____

_____

_____

_____

Indians of the North Pacific Coast: The Potlatch

Along the northwest coast of North America only a narrow strip of land runs between the Pacific Ocean and the heavily wooded mountains. Here the sea, rivers and forests provide an abundance of food. There are land and sea fowl, bear, deer, sea mammals, fish and shellfish. The climate is mild, although rainy, and the Native American people who settled there relied on hunting, fishing and gathering to supply all of their subsistence needs.

Although the richness of the forests and sea brought prosperity to the region, it also brought war. Every inch of ground and coastal waters was owned. Only those families with ownership rights could hunt, fish or gather there. As there was such a small amount of land and so many people who wanted it, fighting was common. They built huge warships from which bows and arrows and even paddles were used as weapons. In close battle, warriors fought with knives, daggers and spears.

Although these people were warlike, however, they were not able to attain status by their deeds of valor or bravery in battle. There were four social grades: slave (captured from other tribes), commoner, noble and chief. These gradations in rank were attained by descent, and wealth was needed to uphold them. Wealth included not only a person's possessions, but also his inherited rights. Inherited rights comprised fishing, hunting and other territorial rights. They also included such things as the right to practice carving and other crafts and the right to say certain prayers. Although the accumulation of goods was necessary, the goods themselves did not give status; it was upon the recognized possession of rights conferring honor and respect that status was based. These rights were linked with certain inheritable names. The names could not be used, however, until they were publicly taken at an intervillage celebration known as a potlatch. To use a name before it was officially taken was considered shameful and to call someone by a name not taken was insulting.

Potlatches were also given to announce important events, such as the accession of an heir to a deceased predecessor, the marriage of a high ranking person, the completion of a house, or the raising of a totem pole. Another reason to give a potlatch was to reestablish dignity and respect after a humiliation or to avenge a public insult.

Potlatches were elaborate ceremonial occasions of feasting and distribution of gifts by the host and his kinsmen to invited guests of other tribes or lineages. The purpose was for the host to impress everyone with his wealth by showing that he could afford to give away many possessions. After feasting, the guests were given furs, blankets, carved dishes and any other goods the host was able to accumulate. Sometimes, especially at face-saving and vengeance potlatches, a host destroyed property to show how little it meant to him. When the potlatch was over, the host was usually impoverished; however, he was secure in the knowledge that he would soon be repaid at the potlatches of others!

1. One of the objects often given away or destroyed at potlatches was the "copper." Its only known purpose is as a symbol of wealth. Draw a copper using appropriate designs. (C, AP)

A Potlatch Copper

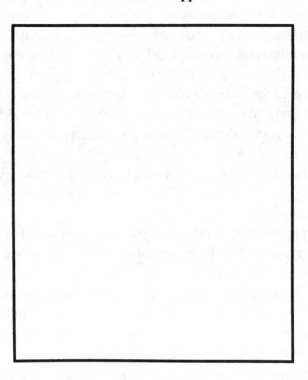

2. Draw a map that shows where at least five tribes of the North Pacific Coast lived. (K, AP)

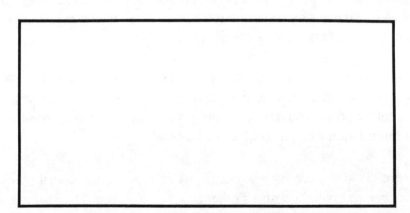

3. Pretend that it is customary for the President of the United States to hold potlatch-type ceremonies. You have been asked to invite the guests and to prepare a list of gifts to be given out according to rank. Make a guest list of fifteen to twenty-five dignitaries from other nations. Decide what gifts should be given to each. (S, E)

4. Many tribes of the North Pacific Coast carved and painted posts, which we call "totem poles." The right to carve totem poles was inherited. The designs themselves belonged to the family who owned the pole. If the artist made any mistakes, he would be disgraced. A totem pole recorded the owner's claim to fame: his ancestry, his wealth and his standing in the town. Make a model totem pole. (C, AP)

Caste

Caste is the most complex, most rigid of all systems of social stratification. It is based upon unequal distribution of goods and power. An individual's relationship to the technology and economic system is determined by the status of his or her caste. All members of a caste share more or less the same social position, behavior and lifestyle. Each caste is assigned certain ritual observances that intensify the awareness of the separateness of the caste groups. Strict rules govern the behavior of the members of one caste group toward those of other castes.

Caste systems are associated with societies in which productive goods are controlled by a relatively small group of political and/or religious leaders. Ethnic castes are often achieved through warfare. One group conquers and subordinates another; the conquered peoples become a socially inferior caste and the conquerors a socially superior caste. Foreign immigrants who are barred from equal privileges also form a socially inferior ethnic caste. Some systems have pariah castes, or hereditary occupational groups which are treated as outcasts.

1. The Eta, an example of a pariah caste, is at the lowest level of the traditional Japanese social system. Although the group has varied origins, most of the Eta in medieval times were butchers, tanners and leather workers. Analyze the possible reasons for their low status. (C, AN)

_____

_____

_____

The Caste System of India

The most complex and refined caste system in the world is the caste system of India. It is based upon the belief that four varna castes came from primordial man: the Brahmins, the Kashatriyas, the Vaishyas and the Shudras. These four varna castes are all clean and unpolluted, but the first three are the purest because their male members are "twice born." The twice-born wear a sacred thread over their shoulders. The Brahmins become the priests, the Kashatriyas the warriors, the Vaishyas the tradesmen and the Shudras the warriors. At the bottom of this system are the polluted and untouchable harijan castes. Each caste refuses to drink water or eat food handled by a member of a lower caste. If a person does so accidentally, he or she must be ritually cleansed or the entire caste is in danger of becoming defiled.

Each of the varna and harijan castes are further subdivided into specific castes, known as "jatis." Members of a jati share certain things in common: the same degree of pollution or purity; whether or not they wear the sacred thread; what kinds of food they may eat; the amount of education they receive; and a set of occupations from which they may choose. There are over 1,000 jatis. Like the more general varna and harijan castes, these jatis are hereditary and endogamous (members must marry within their own jatis).

In this social system marked by such a high degree of social stratification, it is only natural that exchange of goods take the form of redistribution. It is known as the jajmani system. Each jati serves one or more jajman to whom he or she has an obligation to contribute his or her labor or products. In return, the jajmans redistribute a part of the goods they receive to the caste members who serve them. Each collects his share in order of class rank.

The Indian Constitution of 1950 abolished caste "untouchability" and forbade restriction of public facilities on the basis of caste membership); nevertheless, in the rural villages (in which the majority of Indians live) the caste system still persists. Although most caste members no longer strictly adhere to the specific hereditary roles, they still engage in roles considered appropriate to their caste.

2. The Law of Karma states that an individual's caste status is determined by his or her acts in former incarnations. His or her next reincarnation will be determined by present acts. Suppose you believed in reincarnation. Think about the acts you have performed in your present life. Based upon those acts, what will you be in your next reincarnation? Will you be a member of a higher or a lower caste than the one to which you now belong? Draw a sketch and explain. (AP, AN)

_____

_____

_____

_____

_____

_____

_____

_____

_____

3. Write your opinion of the Indian caste system: first from the point of view of a twice-born member of one of the varna castes and then from the point of view of a member of a harijan caste. (AN, E)

Mating and Marriage

Marriage is a set of cultural patterns that define and regulate the relations of a husband and wife to each other, to their kinfolk, to their offspring and to the society of which they are a part. Its major functions are the care and rearing of children, the maintenance of the household and the provision of the other cultural needs of the family. In fact, in most societies marriages are arranged by the couple's families or at least involve family consent. Although marriages are expected to last forever, most societies provide for some type of divorce for those which do not succeed.

All societies have systems which designate those people with whom mating is preferred and those with whom mating is prohibited. The prohibition of sexual relations between certain close relatives, known as the incest taboo, is universal. Parent-child and brother-sister taboo is found everywhere. The few exceptions in the brother-sister taboo involve royal lineages in order for them to retain their divinity. Incest taboo is usually extended beyond the nuclear family. Most include cousins, especially those classified by the same terminology as brothers and sisters. For example, in some societies all female cousins are referred to by the same word that refers to sisters; therefore, the relationships with them are governed by the same rules.

Incest taboo inevitably results in exogamy, the custom or law that requires people to marry outside a certain social group to which they belong. Exogamy is helpful in that it enlarges the social and economic base of the kinship groups involved. It encourages reciprocal bonds between the two groups.

A few societies have systems of endogamy. Endogamous rule requires, or at least encourages, people to marry within a certain group to which they belong—usually a larger group, such as a descent group, an association, an ethnic group, a social group or a caste. Endogamy is based upon the desire to retain the exclusive characteristics of the group.

Some societies have systems which provide for affinal, or continuation, marriages. The three basic forms of affinal marriage are the levirate, the sororate and the extended affinal marriage. A levirate is the marriage of a woman to her husband's brother upon her husband's death. A sororate is the marriage of a man to his wife's sister upon his wife's death. An extended affinal marriage is the marriage of a man or woman to his or her spouse's kin other than a sibling when a sibling is not available; however, this form of marriage is not very common.

1. Although incest taboo seems to be based upon social rather than biological principles, most scientists agree that there are positive genetic effects. Use Mendel's law to explain the dangers of "inbreeding." (C, AP)

_____

_____

_____

2. Parallel cousins are those cousins whose related parents are the same sex. Cross cousins are those whose related parents are the opposite sex. In most societies that distinguish between these two types of cousins, mating with a parallel cousin is taboo. Exceptions are the parallel-cousin marriages among patrilineal pastoralists such as traditional Arabic Muslims and the Muslims of India and Pakistan. Analyze the reasons patrilineal pastoralists might prefer parallel-cousin marriages. (C, AN)

_____

_____

_____

3. In most societies marriages are arranged by a couple's families. In many nonliterate societies the bride's family expects a bride price, or progeny price, to be paid by the groom's kin. It is a compensation for future offspring and is common in societies where children belong to the father's kinship group. In a few societies suitor service is an alternative. The potential groom works for his intended wife's family. Cite an example in the Old Testament in which a man served his uncle for fourteen years in return for the right to marry his uncle's daughter. (K, C)

_____

_____

4. Anthropologists classify three types of husband-wife relationships: monogamy, polygyny and polyandry. Define each. Speculate as to why monogamy is the prevailing form even in societies that permit or encourage polygamy (either polygyny or polyandry). (C, AN)

Monogamy:_____

_____

Polygyny: _____

_____

Polyandry: _____

_____

The Nuclear Family

The family is a group of individuals united by bonds of kinship. They interact with each other according to the behavioral patterns of their culture. Although all societies have family groupings, the forms these groupings take vary greatly. The reason for these variations is that they are shaped by cultural needs rather than biological needs. In general, the family serves four basic functions: the establishment of acceptable behavior patterns regarding mating and the establishment of legal parents for children; the nurture and enculturation of those children; the organization of a division of labor between spouses; and the establishment of relationships of descent and kinship.

Kinship charts are drawn to represent relationships of family members. Circles represent females and triangles represent males. Double horizontal lines are drawn to indicate a marriage relationship. Single vertical lines connect one generation to the next. Single horizontal lines indicate sibling relationships.

A: Husband/father
B: Wife/mother
C: Daughter/sister
D: Son/brother

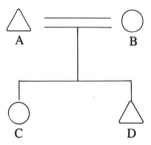

1. The above kinship chart represents a nuclear family. The nuclear family is the group composed of one set of parents and their children (born or adopted) and no other relatives. Draw a kinship chart of your nuclear family. (C, AP)

Every person who establishes a family is a member of two nuclear, or conjugal-natal, families: the family into which he or she was born (also known as the natal family or family of orientation) and the family he or she founds with a spouse upon marriage (also known as the conjugal family or family of procreation). These two families are similar in terms of form and function; however, the statuses of the individuals within the families are different.

2. Complete this analogy:

   Conjugal : Family of Procreation :: Natal : _____

3. Draw a kinship chart that represents your mother's conjugal-natal family. Draw overlapping circles to indicate her conjugal and her natal family and label each. (C, AP)

4. The simple conjugal-natal family is only possible when the marriage is monogamous. If there are more than one husband (very rare) or wife at one time, the result is a composite conjugal-natal family. The spouse with more than one mate usually maintains a separate relationship with each and with their offspring. Draw a kinship chart that designates a composite conjugal-natal family based upon sororal polygyny, the simultaneous marriage of one husband to two or more sisters. (C, AP)

5. What are the benefits of polygyny to women? (AN)

_____

_____

_____

_____

Residence Patterns

Once a couple marries, where they live is usually determined by the preferred residence pattern of their culture. When the married couple lives in or near the husband's natal residence, it is called a "virilocal" or "patrilocal" residence rule. If the couple settles in or near the wife's natal residence, it is called "uxorilocal" or "matrilocal." In some societies the couple settles in or near the residence of the husband's mother's brother; this type of residence pattern is called "avunculocal." If the couple has the choice of living near either parental home, it is called "bilocal" or "ambilocal." When the newly married couple sets up residency without much reference to the residence of either's conjugal-natal family, it is called "neolocal." Although one of these five basic rules usually prevails as the ideal, there is often a great deal of variation within the society.

1. Neolocal residence is the most frequent in societies with advanced technology and economic systems. Evaluate its possible effect upon the stability of those marriages. (AN, E)

_____

_____

_____

2. Analyze the importance of techno-economic adaptation upon the residence rule that designates the culturally preferred place for a new couple to establish its household. (C, AN)

_____

_____

_____

3. A factor that tempers the effects of residence rules is whether the marriages are based upon village endogamy or exogamy. Draw two cartoons from the point of view of a bride in a society that favors patrilocal residence, first in a village that favors endogamy and then in a village that favors exogamy. (C, AP, AN, S)

4. The extended family is the common residence of two or more families (monogamous or polygamous) with a biological link. Usually each nuclear or polygamous family functions as a distinct unit within the larger extended family. An extended family rule may be patrilocal, matrilocal, bilocal or avunculocal. Analyze the benefits of an extended family. (AN)

_____

_____

_____

_____

Kinship Groups

Although the basic unit of kinship is the conjugal-natal, or nuclear, family, that unit must be seen as a part of a larger network of kinship organization: bilateral, or cognatic kinship, known as the kindred; ambilineal (or nonunilineal) kinship, known as the ramage; unilineal kinship, which may be either matrilineal or patrilineal and which takes the form of a lineage, a clan, a moiety, or a phratry; and double descent, which is also known as dual, duolineal or double unilineal descent.

BILATERAL, OR COGNATIC KINSHIP: THE KINDRED—The kindred reckons descent from both parents and potentially includes everyone who can be traced as related; as a functionary unit, however, limits are placed (e.g., second or third cousin).

AMBILINEAL KINSHIP: THE RAMAGE—The members of a ramage trace their descent from a common ancestor, either patrilineally or matrilineally. Ramages, which are quite rare, usually have a corporate quality; they own land and other goods and can transmit them to rightful members. Membership in a ramage has a definite advantage and is strictly limited both by genealogical ties and the requisite fulfillment of obligations to the ramage. Of the few ramages that exist, most are Oceanic.

UNILINEAL DESCENT: THE LINEAGE—The lineage is the simplest type of unilineal descent. It is composed of all consanguineous kin (related by blood) that share a common ancestor; this ancestor is a real person. In the case of a patrilineage, the ancestor is a male; in the case of a matrilineage, the ancestor is a female.

UNILINEAL DESCENT: THE CLAN—The main difference between a clan and a lineage is that the common ancestor upon whom a lineage is based is known and the common ancestor upon whom a clan is based is remote and often mythical. Clans are usually exogamous.

UNILINEAL DESCENT: THE PHRATRY—A phratry, which is relatively rare, is the uniting of two or more clans that share a remote common ancestor or common ceremonial activities. They are also exogamous.

DOUBLE DESCENT—This rare form of kinship organization is the coexistence of matrilineal and patrilineal descent systems within the same society. Those that exist are found in Oceanic and African societies.

1. The kindred may be said to be an ego-centered group. Explain. (K, C)

_____

_____

_____

2. In most societies, the kinship bond is stronger than all others. Is this true of your society? Do you think most members of your society tend to depend upon their relatives for security, or do they depend upon others? Do you think these things will change? Explain your answers. (AN)

_____

_____

_____

3. Most human societies are based upon the principle of unilineal descent. What is the primary advantage of this form of descent? (AN, E)

_____

_____

_____

4. Although bilateral descent is not widespread, the bilateral tracing of descent, at least as far as the four grandparents, occurs in all societies. What varies is the importance attached to this bilateral descent in the organization of the member's life and in the organization of the community. How important are bilateral descent and the resulting groups of close consanguineous (related by blood) kinsmen in your life? In the organization of your community? (AN, E)

_____

_____

_____

5. Consanguineous is the term used to describe kinship based upon common descent; consanguineous relatives are also called blood relatives. Affinal is the term used to describe kinship based upon marriage. List five of your relatives related by consanguinity and five related by affinity. (C, AP)

Consanguineous Kin

1.

2.

3.

4.

5.

Affinal Kin

1.

2.

3.

4.

5.

Kinship Terms

Kinship terms, or the set of names used to symbolize various kinship statuses, reflect the kinship grouping in the social organization of a culture. No system can distinguish every separate genealogical relationship. Instead, some are lumped together into categories. A kinship term that merges lineal, or direct, relatives (such as one's father or mother) with collateral, or indirect, relatives (such as one's father's brother or one's mother's sister) is called "classificatory." A kinship term that applies to only one genealogical distinction (such as mother and father being used exclusively for actual parents) is called "descriptive" or "particularizing." Because kinship terms designate social statuses, what you call a person should also determine your behavior toward that person.

Comanche Kinship Terminology

The following account of the Comanche kinship system is based upon the study done by anthropologist E. Adamson Hoebel. The Comanche social structure is bilateral; individuals belong equally to the kindred of both parents. It is also bilocal; the newly married couple has free choice of whether to settle with or near the bride's or groom's parents. Although polygamy is now forbidden by the federal law of the United States, until that law went into effect, polygamy was permitted. The kindred is exogamous within a specified relationship.

A Comanche male calls his mother *pia,* but the term is not exclusively reserved for her. He also calls other female relatives *pia:* his mother's sisters, his mother's female cousins and his father's brother's wife. In other words, *pia* designates any "female relative of my mother's generation and of my mother's and my father's kindred."

A Comanche male also lumps together "male relatives of his father's generation and of his father's and his mother's kindred." The term *ap'* may be used to designate not only his father, but also his father's brothers, his father's male cousins and his mother's sister's husband.

The Comanche does have descriptive, or particularizing terms for both his mother's brother and his father's sister. His mother's brother is called *ara.* His father's sister is called *paha.* This system of lumping together the father and paternal uncle and mother and paternal aunt while distinguishing the maternal uncle and paternal aunt is called bifurcate, or forked, merging.

The Comanche male uses the same terms to designate brother and sister that he uses to designate all relatives of his own generation. He does distinguish between the relative ages, however. The term *paBi* is used to designate any older male relative of his generation: his older brother, his father's brother's son, his father's sister's son, his mother's brother's son, his mother's sister's son or his wife's sister's husband. If these same relatives were younger than he, he would use the term *tami* to refer to them. The elder female relatives of his generation are called *patsi* and the younger ones are called *nami.*

In a similar way, the term *tua* would not only refer to his son, but also to the male offspring of the *paBi* and *tami,* the sons of his wife's sisters and his sister's daughter's husband. *Pedi* lumps together his own female offspring with the female offspring of his *patsi* and *nami,* his wife's sister's daughters and his sister's son's wife.

All of these terms would be different for a Comanche female!

1. Label Ego's generation and the generation of his parents in the kinship chart below. Ego is a Comanche male. (K, C, AP)

Remember:
   ◯ : Female
   △ : Male
   | : Separates generations
   = : Marriage
   — : Siblings

Ego: The hypothetical person used as the reference point for analyzing kinship relations.

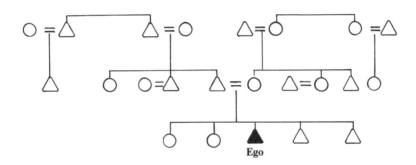

2. Compare and contrast Anglo-American kinship terminology with Comanche kinship terminology. (C, AN)

_____

_____

_____

3. Think of at least five alternate terms in Anglo-American kinship terminology used to designate the relationships of mother and father. Label the most respectful and the least respectful. (C, E)

Mother: **Father:**

Associations and Age Groups

Kinship is the basis of the social organization of every society; nevertheless, many societies have groups, or associations, that cut across kinship lines. Rarely do they replace kinship ties, but rather they complement or extend them. If the association includes all members of a certain age range, it is called an "age-grade," "age-class" or "age-set" association.

Age Groups

The use of age as a basis of status identification is universal; nevertheless, age groups, or associations of men or women of a similar age range, do not usually have a great impact on the organization of a society. Although they may complement or extend kinship ties, they are not usually central to the organization of community life or to the structure and function of the political system. Exceptions, however, are found among certain Native American tribes of the North American Plains and several African systems.

The Nuer

The Nuer are an East African people who live in scattered regions on the banks of the Nile in the southern Sudan. Their subsistence is dependent upon the raising of cattle, but they supplement their meat and milk diet by the cultivation of millet and the spearing of fish. During the rainy season when their lands are flooded, they remain in permanent villages built on high ground.

In each tribal area the males are banded together into six age sets. At puberty, a boy is initiated into the set with which he will be affiliated. The initiation includes the cutting of six deep scars running from ear to ear across his forehead. All boys initiated during a six-year period are members of the same set. Then there are no initiations for four years, at the end of which a new set is formed.

Marriage is polygynous. To mark it, the groom's family gives cattle to the bride's kin—both paternal and maternal. It is believed essential that every man have at least one heir; therefore, if a man dies unmarried, one of his kin marries in his name. Their children are considered the deceased man's.

Kinship ties are very important. Each maximal, or main, lineage is divided into two secondary lineages; they are divided into four tertiary lineages, which are divided into eight minimal lineages. There is much intratribal fighting among the Nuer. If the fighting is contained within one tertiary segment, it remains a local matter. If more than one tertiary segment is involved, the minimal segments of each tertiary segment join together. If two secondary segments of a lineage quarrel, the four minimal (two tertiary) of each secondary segment join together. All eight minimal segments join together as a maximal lineage against any other maximal lineage.

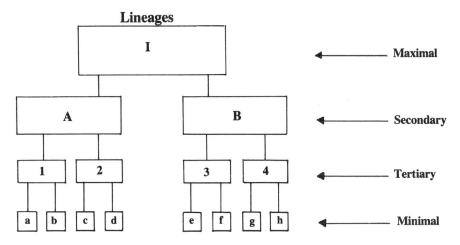

Lineages

- Maximal
- Secondary
- Tertiary
- Minimal

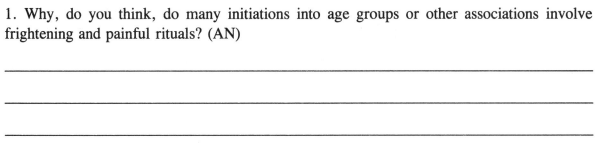

1. Why, do you think, do many initiations into age groups or other associations involve frightening and painful rituals? (AN)

_____

_____

_____

2. Some Native American tribes of the North American Plains have a system of associations graded in a prestige hierarchy from young to old. Research and report on one of these age-graded associations. (C, AP)

Innovations in technology and the quickened culture change that accompanies them often cause changes in the social organization as well.

3. Analyze the effects of migration (for example, from rural to urban areas) associated with changing technological and economic conditions upon the increased importance of associations. (C, AN)

_____

_____

_____

_____

4. Many associations that used to admit males only now admit women members. Analyze the reasons for the change. Interview some ''old'' members and some ''new'' members, both male and female. Do their feelings on the subject differ? Summarize the results of your interviews. (AN)

_____

_____

_____

Political Organization

Every society has the need to maintain internal social order and to regulate its relations with other societies. The form which the political system takes depends a great deal upon the economic and technological development of the society. The units of structure upon which it is organized may be territorial, kinship, and/or associational in nature.

The simplest form of political organization, characteristic of nomadic hunter-gatherers, is a "band." A band is a small, territorially-based social group whose members are usually related. Primitive farmers and herders are more likely to have more complex, "multicentric authority systems." In these systems authority is still kinship based; however, it is also based upon seniority within the descent system. When necessary (for example, when the entire community is threatened), a more centralized form of authority system may emerge, but it is usually temporary. The most complex form, the centralized authority system, is characteristic of advanced farmers, herders who have dominated subject peoples and, of course, industrialized societies. In this system power is concentrated in the hands of a very few people; furthermore, authority is based upon associational ties rather than kinship ties. When a government in the form of a centralized authority directs and organizes social policy in behalf of the whole society, the association has become a state.

1. Make a poster or a collage that illustrates the functions of government. (C, AP)

2. The word *monarchy* stems from two Greek words: *monos,* meaning "single" and *arkhein,* meaning "to rule." Evaluate this statement: The word *monarchy* is a misnomer. (C, AN, E)

_____

_____

_____

Law and Social Control

Every society has a system of social control that encourages some behavior and discourages other behavior. Law is part of that system of social control. There are certain features that characterize law: the legitimate use or threat of physical or economic coercion; a privileged party to apply the coercion in a specified manner; and regularity, or predictability (although not certainty).

3. Which of the three basic characteristics of law is shared with custom? (C)

_____

_____

_____

The !Kung:* Bands

At one time the !Kung and other Bushmen were widespread throughout eastern and southern Africa; however, their population and the extent of their territories have steadily decreased. By the 1980's there were less than twenty bands, averaging about twenty members each. All the members of a band are related by blood or marriage and they live and work together by hunting or gathering. The territory of each band includes a waterhole and is large enough so that it may be efficiently exploited.

Wild foods within one's territory are considered free goods until they are killed or collected. The first to strike a large animal with his arrow is in charge of the distribution of the meat. Also, the hunters may move freely into those territories of bands to which they are related. The groups are patrilocal and exogamous, with the young girls usually marrying into bands in adjacent territories; therefore, each band is related to most neighboring bands by marriage.

In cases of dispute between band members, they usually call upon the headman for advice. He is also consulted when important decisions must be made, such as the choice of a new campsite or whether or not to allow a distant band to partake of their water supply. Although his word is usually heeded, his power is limited. The headman, whose role is hereditary, also acts as custodian of the land and food sources; however, neither he nor his family receives any tribute or special honors.

The !Kung have little contact with members of distant bands. Occasionally, however, !Kung strangers meet. The elder stranger first finds out the name of the other and addresses him with a kinship term he uses for a relative with that name. (Because there are only a few !Kung names, it is certain that the elder man has had a relative with the same name.) The younger man responds with the corresponding term. For example, if the elder man calls the younger man ''uncle,'' the younger man calls the older man ''nephew.''

4. Analyze the reasons for the steady decline in the population and territory of the !Kung. (AN)

_____

_____

_____

_____

_____

_____

*The ''!'' represents an implosive clicking sound characteristic of Bushman languages.

Trial by ~~Jury~~ Song

The social organization of the Eskimos is based upon the bilateral family. There are no lineages, clans, clubs or governments. Each group, which seldom exceeds one hundred members, has a headman; however, the headman has neither legal nor judicial authority. Before outside law was imposed upon them, certain forms of homicide were allowed: infanticide, invalidicide, suicide and senilicide. There is no land ownership and free borrowing of goods is customary; therefore, there are few legal offenses against property.

Nevertheless, there is an aggressive status struggle among the men. It is manifested in the competition of hunting skills and in wife stealing. Although wife stealing is not a crime, the man whose wife is stolen is not expected to let the act go unchallenged. If he kills the wife stealer, he will not be punished. If he himself is killed in the attempt, however, eventually his murder will have to be avenged by his family. In any case, it is customary for an Eskimo man to marry the widow and adopt the children of the man he has killed.

There are alternatives to killing a wife stealer or other aggressor. The injured man might challenge his opponent to a wrestling or hitting match. He might also challenge him to a song contest!

If a man challenges an aggressor and if the aggressor accepts his challenge, the "duel" begins. The injured man composes an insulting song which mocks and ridicules his opponent and his family and accuses him of various misdeeds. He recites his song loudly to the wild accompaniment of drums. When he has finished, his opponent sings a similar song aimed at the challenger. They exchange songs in this manner until the matter is settled; it may last for days or even continue in intervals for years! The one who receives the most applause is the winner. Who was right or wrong is not established, but the matter is settled without other hostilities.

5. Predict what might happen years later if a man whose wife was stolen is killed in his attempt to challenge the theft and if the wife stealer adopts the man's son. (C, AN)

_____

_____

_____

_____

6. Write an insulting song that you might sing to a person who has just stolen and crashed your new automobile or who has injured you in some other way. (S)

Ideology and Religion

Ideology is a universal aspect of culture; every culture has a system of beliefs that explains the people's existence and their relation to others, to the world and to the universe as they perceive it. Although most ideologies are based upon belief in supernatural beings, some are not.

Religion is an ordered system of ideas, objects, norms, myths and rituals which carry important meanings for the people who believe in them. This body of knowledge concerning the nature of the world acts as a guide which tells the people how to act in various circumstances. The most basic aspect of religion is "animism," or the belief in supernatural beings. These beings may be in the form of gods, devils, angels, ghosts, fairies, witches and so on.

Another basic component of many religions is "mana." Mana is a belief in the supernatural attribute, or quality, of persons and things. It is an impersonal force that may be transferred from one person or object to another. Mana is used to account for events which are otherwise unexplainable. (For example, a spear that spears an extraordinary number of fish would be believed to possess mana in systems in which mana is an important attribute.) Although mana is an attribute of many belief systems, it is most prevalent in Melanesia. It is believed that one comes to possess mana by touching an object that has mana. The mana can be used for benign or malevolent purposes, but is itself neither good nor evil.

1. In your society, what would most people believe to be the reason for more fish being speared? (C, AN)

_____

_____

_____

2. Are there any objects which you believe to possess mana? For example, have you every carried a rabbit's foot or a four-leaf clover? Create a cartoon about a time when you or someone you know carried or wore an object because it possessed mana. (C, S)

3. Make a poster of items believed by some members of your society to possess mana. (C, AP)

4. Write an original short story about a person who believes mana is responsible for his/her achievements. For example, you might write about a baseball player who believes that his/her bat has mana or about a writer who believes his/her pen has mana. (C, AP, S)

World View

The way in which members of a culture perceive their total environment is known as their world view. When seen by an outsider, one who is not completely enculturated in the culture being studied, this view is called "etic." When seen from the point of view of an insider, the view is called "emic."

The Navajo World View

Fundamental to most systems of belief are creation myths that explain the origins of the world and the people's relation to it. The Navajo origin myth tells of Holy People, supernatural beings who abide in the sacred part of the world, and Earth Surface People, the ordinary human beings (living and dead). It tells that from time immemorial the universe has been a very dangerous place, inhabited by people who should not be trusted. The only people to trust are living relatives. The greatest worry are witches in the form of werewolves and ghouls; although anyone may be a witch, those who are too prosperous are especially suspect. Upon death, people become vengeful ghosts who harass the living; they are feared by children and adults alike.

The universe is viewed as an orderly, interrelated system of cause and effect. Their basic quest is for harmony, for when there is disharmony, catastrophe and personal illness result. In fact, illness is the surest sign of disharmony; that is why elaborate ceremonies are held in order to cure sickness, both physical and mental, and to protect people on dangerous missions. As part of the ceremonies, their myths are chanted. They involve the gods of the wind, rain, dawn, sun, semiprecious stones, corn, tobacco, squash and the bean. While the myths are being chanted, a sand painter creates a sand painting. He drops dry pigments made of pollen, flower petals, charcoal or powdered stone onto a bed of clean sand. The sick person sits in the middle of the painting. Pinches of the painting are believed to enter the patient's body and cure it. The painting must be destroyed by sunset of the day it is begun.

Except for witches, people and things are neither inherently good nor inherently evil. The goal is to keep the good and evil in balance and to avoid taking risks which might upset that balance. For example, contact with strangers is avoided. If a stranger appears, a nine-day chant is recited in order to restore harmony.

1. Compare and contrast the world view of the Navajo with the world view of another Native American people. (C, AN)

_____

_____

_____

_____

_____

_____

_____

2. Why is it difficult to write a world view for the people of the United States? What generalizations can be made regarding America's world view? (C, AN)

_____

_____

_____

_____

_____

3. Write a world view of a subgroup of your society of which you are a member. Does it differ from the society on a whole in any way? (C, AN, S, E)

_____

_____

_____

_____

_____

_____

_____

_____

Mythology

Myths are primitive accounts of the origin, character and functions of the ancient gods, of the origin of humankind and of the condition of the visible world. The time in which these events occur is completely different from our time frame.

In primitive cultures it is only natural for the people to have a sense of awe in the presence of the wonder of nature. They attribute to these objects—the sun, sky, sea, mountains, etc.—a free will and personality similar to that of humans. As they consider themselves inferior to these objects, they believe the objects to have an even greater freedom, personality and power than they.

1. Most ideologies include creation myths, or myths of origin. According to Hawaiian mythology, the Heavens and Earth were created by Kane, the chief god, with the help of Ku, Lono and Kanaloa. Research the myth and draw a picture that illustrates the way Hawaiians perceive the creation of the world. (C, AP)

2. Research and summarize a Greek myth of origin. Illustrate your summary. (C, AP)

Ritual

Accompanying a people's system of belief is usually a set of actions or ritual observances. Sometimes the ritual is in the form of sacrifice of a valued thing in the hopes it will please the supernatural being. Abstention is another common ritual. Many peoples give up specific foods, either at all times or during certain periods, in the belief that eating those foods would offend the supernatural being in which they believe. The observance of taboos, or the avoidance of activities prohibited by the supernatural beings, is another type of ritual intended to improve thier relation to the forces that control their destinies. Taboo is sometimes associated with totemism, or the belief that an animal, plant or place is supernaturally related to a certain descent group. Prayer is another ritual action through which people attempt to influence the supernatural being in which they believe.

1. Judge the importance of ritual. (C, AN, E)

_____

_____

_____

_____

2. Taboo is a negative element, consisting of a set of negative rules. If those rules are broken, the breaker is punished by the supernatural force. Analyze the functions of taboo. (C, AN)

_____

_____

_____

_____

3. Most religions have religious specialists. Compare and contrast a priest and a shaman. (C, AN)

_____

_____

_____

_____

Magic and Sorcery

Magic, like religion, is based upon a belief in the supernatural. In religion, however, the individuals believe the supernatural powers to be superior to themselves; although they do their best to influence those powers to react in a helpful way, they are still subject to the whim of those powers. On the other hand, magicians believe that they are capable of controlling those powers if they follow certain formulas. Magic is not necessarily used for evil purposes, but when it is, it is called sorcery.

1. Most people in modern societies do not believe in magic, and yet magic often appears to work. Analyze the reasons for the apparent success of magic. (C, AN)

_____

_____

_____

_____

_____

Ghost Cults and Ancestor Worship

Although an awareness of ghosts exists in most cultures, the amount of concern over the activity and feeling of the ghosts varies. When the concern is intense, ancestor worship is common. Ancestral spirits are believed to be especially concerned with relations within the kinship group. Ancestor worship is usually associated with social conservatism; when individuals do not conform to the old standards, they are punished by religious sanctions.

2. People who believe their dead to be active and useful members of the community generally have feelings about death that are different from those of a people who perceive death as a finality. Explain. (C, AN)

_____

_____

_____

_____

The Arts

Art is a universal aspect of culture; however, although aesthetic (pertaining to a sense of the beautiful) expression of some type occurs in every known culture, art for art's sake is rare in most societies. Art usually involves the modifications of useful objects or ideas. These modifications do not add to the usefulness of the objects or ideas; rather they are meant to bring satisfaction to the producer and the beholder. It is this aesthetic quality, over and above any usefulness or symbolic content, which classifies an activity as art.

Art takes many forms. It is the formal product of any activity that produces or arranges sounds, colors, forms, movements or other elements in a way designed to affect one's sense of beauty. Art may be naturalistic or abstract, or a combination of both. The impressions may be conveyed through any medium: graphic or plastic forms, written or oral literature, drama, dance, religious ceremonies, architecture and so on. Even forms of personal adornment, such as clothing and tatooing, are types of aesthetic expression.

The art of non-literate peoples is usually referred to as primitive art. Its main function is to reflect and reinforce the value scheme of the culture. Unlike the modern artist who develops a personal style, the primitive artist works with a very structured set of rules and media with which to ensure the proper response from his audience. Art in these societies plays an important role in maintaining the solidarity of the society.

Art has a very close relation to ideology, especially in terms of religion. Because religion is subjective, its concepts need to be presented in an objective manner so that they seem more real and convincing. Art is the medium through which this is accomplished. Especially important is the representation of gods and spirits. Masks are often used to portray these supernatural beings. Another common medium of religious art is statuary. It is important in Melanesia, Polynesia, Central America and especially Africa. African statues are created to house the spirits of the dead ancestors. Once a spirit moves into a statue, the statue gains a supernatural quality. The human ancestor, as represented by the object, now has godlike powers.

1. The term ''primitive art'' is considered a misnomer by many anthropologists. Choose a viewpoint and prepare your closing remarks for a debate on the subject. (C, AN, E)

_____

_____

_____

_____

_____

_____

2. On brown paper, paint a mural in the style of a prehistoric cave painting. Have it tell about an event, real or imaginary. (C, AP. S)

3. Research the art style of the Native Americans living along the northwest Pacific Coast. Decorate a box in that style. Choose figures that have some meaning in your life and explain what the figures represent. (C, AP, S, E)

4. Masks are important in many Native American ceremonies. Members of the False Face Societies of the Iroquois tribes wore False Fase Masks to drive away evil spirits and to cure the sick. They were carved from a living tree to give them life. After being cut from the tree, a mask was painted: red, if cut in the morning; black, if cut in the afternoon. Draw a picture of a False Face Mask. (C, AP)

5. Describe the characteristics of African statuary. (C, AP)

_____

_____

_____

6. Create a poster that illustrates forms of verbal art. (C, AP)

7. Like other forms of art, music and dance are also aspects of culture and, as such, function in several ways. They may serve as a source of pure pleasure or as a means of emotional release for the composer, performer, viewer and/or listener. Music is often part of the social, political and religious ceremonies of the society. Describe a ceremony or ritual observance (from the culture of your choice) in which music or dance plays an important part. (C, AP, AN)

_____

_____

_____

_____

_____

Language and Other Ways to Communicate

Language is a uniquely human phenomenon. Although other animals use sounds and gestures to communicate, only humans combine them in the highly structured manner we call language. Language is an aspect of culture—it must be learned; furthermore, culture could not exist without language.

Although some languages may be thought of as more advanced than others because of the adaptations they have undergone, no language should be thought of as a more complete system than another. Each language fulfills the needs of the culture of which it is a part.

Linguistic anthropologists are becoming more and more concerned with the ways in which language, culture and society are related. These recent concerns have led to three relatively new subfields of linguistic anthropology: ethnolinguistics, or the study of how language affects the thought patterns of the individuals of a given culture; ethnosemantics, or the study of the meanings found in each society; and the ethnology of speaking, in which the principal concerns are speech as a cultural behavior and the cultural rules that govern that behavior.

1. It was stated above that culture could not exist without language. Do you agree or disagree? Tell why. (AP, AN, E)

_____

_____

_____

2. Linguists divide the world's languages into stocks, or families. English is included in the Indo-European family of languages. Make a chart that shows the nine subgroups of Indo-European languages. Include examples of each. (C, AP)

Language Structure

A language's structure may be divided into three separate aspects: its phonology, or sound system; its grammar, or system of organizing the sounds into morphemes (the smallest meaningful linguistic units); and its lexicon, or basic words and their meanings.

3. The branch of grammar dealing with the formation of phrases and sentences is called syntax. Languages which are very dependent upon morphology can have a more relaxed syntax. Compare a language in which morphology is important with one in which syntax is the essential feature. (C, AN)

_____

_____

_____

4. Create a cartoon or comic strip in which a foreigner who has recently arrived in the United States unknowingly uses an incorrect syntax pattern. (C, AP, S)

Language and Culture

Ethnolinguistics is the study of causal relations between linguistic and cultural forms. Ethnolinguists study the ways in which language pre-conditions how individuals perceive reality and how language structure reflects the culture. They are especially interested in how it reflects the people's adaptation to their particular environment. Two important pioneers in this subfield were anthropologists Edward Sapir and Benjamin Lee Whorf; in fact, the formulation upon which this study is centered is often called the "Sapir-Whorf Hypothesis."

5. Anthropologist Franz Boas first made the observation in the late nineteenth century that Eskimos have a large number of words for snow. This is obviously because their survival is so dependent upon the conditions of the snow. Draw a picture of an American/European sub-culture in which the exact condition of the snow is also important and which also contains a number of words for snow. (C, AP)

6. Cultural rules, as well as grammatical rules, govern our use of language. Fill in the speech bubble in each picture with a form of address appropriate to the situation. (C, AP)

7. A person's name is often determined by his or her position in the society. Make a list of the names you have had. What names might you have in the future? What status does each represent? (K, C, AP)

Past Names & Statuses	Present Names & Statuses	Future Names & Statuses
_____	_____	_____
_____	_____	_____
_____	_____	_____
_____	_____	_____

Other Ways to Communicate

There are several ways to communicate which do not use language. Gestures, facial expressions and even the distance a person puts between himself and another are all modes of learned communication. The understanding of these and other cues of a culture is vital to effective participation in that society.

8. Draw pictures in which you depict the use of body language to denote the indicated feelings or emotions: superiority, fear and distrust. (C, AP, S)

Superiority	Fear	Distrust

9. Writing is a set of techniques for graphically representing speech; it is not language. Compared with language, which is one of the oldest human achievements, writing is a recent innovation. It exists only in advanced societies. Analyze the importance of writing. (C, AN)

_____

_____

_____

_____

Just for Fun!

1. Make a poster that illustrates the applications of anthropology in today's world. (C, AP)

2. Write a letter to the Society for Applied Anthropology. State your view on whether or not it is ethical to intervene in the culture of a society in order to bring about change. (C, AP, AN, E)

3. Create a word search of anthropological terms. (K, AP)

4. Make a flipbook of Native American dwellings. Tell which societies used them and how each suited the society's lifestyle. (C, AP, AN)

5. Analyze the needs and lifestyle of your family and explain whether or not your home fits those needs. (C, AN)

6. Research and report on two different societies in similar geographic environments. Discuss to what extent the environment influences the lifestyle of a society. (C, AN)

7. These five inventions have had an enormous effect upon human societies: fire-making, the wheel, metal-smelting, writing and the true arch. Decide which you feel is the **most** important. Create a bulletin board or table top display to demonstrate its importance. (C, AP, S, E)

8. Did you ever imagine that you lived in another society or at another time in human history? Write an original story in which you find yourself in a different society or in the same society at a different time. (C, AN, S)

9. Describe something that is considered normal in your culture that is not considered normal in another culture (or *vice versa*). (C, AP)

10. One of the best known projects involving applied anthropology is the volunteer organization of the United States called the Peace Corps. Create a recruitment poster for the Peace Corps. (C, AP, AN, S, E)

11. Write an ethnology of a segment of your society of which you now know little. Visit that sub-culture and interview its members. Some examples are: a nursing home, a religious organization or a particular religious ceremony, a police department or a hospital. (C, AP, AN, S, E)

12. Design a poster that illustrates the difference between enculturation and acculturation. (K, C, AP)

Pre-Test

Circle the correct answer.

1. All modern humans belong to this species.

    A. *Homo erectus erectus*   B. *Homo sapiens sapiens*   C. *Homo habilis*

2. The learned behaviors characteristic of a society is its _____.

    A. Culture   B. Role   C. Status

3. The kinship group consisting of an individual, his/her spouse, and their offspring is a _____.

    A. Lineage   B. Nuclear family   C. Clan

4. The rule that requires marriage within a group is _____.

    A. Exogamy   B. Monogamy   C. Endogamy

5. Intensive agriculture developed as a result of this invention.

    A. Wheel   B. Plow   C. Fire

6. Tools in the Paleolithic and Neolithic Ages were made of _____.

    A. Stone   B. Iron   C. Bronze

7. The complex of behavior usually associated with a particular status is a _____.

    A. Society   B. Role   C. Culture

8. Marriage of a man to more than one wife at the same time is _____.

    A. Polygyny   B. Monogamy   C. Polyandry

9. A residence rule in which a couple settles with or near the groom's family is _____.

    A. Bilocal   B. Matrilocal   C. Virilocal

10. A belief in supernatural beings is called _____.

    A. Ideology   B. Linguistics   C. Animism

What Is Anthropology?

1. _____ is the system of learned behavior patterns, beliefs, arts and institutions characteristic of members of a society.

2. _____ is the branch of anthropology that studies the material remains of past cultures.

3. The borrowing of knowledge from other cultures is _____.

4. _____ anthropology is the branch concerned with the genetic characteristics of human populations.

5. _____ focuses upon the sociocultural context of language.

6. In the twentieth century, _____, a German-born American, stressed the importance of fieldwork and first-hand observation.

Human Evolution and Variation

1. _____ is the only existing species of human beings.

2. _____ wrote *Origin of Species.*

3. _____ is the principle that those better adapted to their environment live longer to produce more offspring than those not as well adapted.

4. Humans belong to the order of mammals called _____.

5. A primate with the characteristics of a human being is called _____.

6. Another name for the Old Stone Age is _____.

7. A species is a(n) _____(closed/open) genetic system.

Technology

1. The simplest level of subsistence, or means of obtaining food, is _____.

2. The Shoshone relied principally on _____ to obtain their food.

3. The domestication of plants led to the spread of _____ as a subsistence technique.

4. The domestication of animals led to the spread of _____ as a subsistence technique.

5. The invention of the _____ was greatly responsible for the development of intensive agriculture.

6. According to V.G. Childe, writing, far-reaching trade, arithmetic, geometry and astronomy and a priviledged ruling class are among the characteristics of early _____.

7. Societies dependent upon _____ (agriculture/pastoralism) tend to be the most sedentary.

8. True or False: The only function of clothing in most cultures is to protect the wearer from the elements.

9. The invention of the _____ greatly improved land transportation.

10. (Basketry/Pottery) _____ is better suited to nomadic food-gatherers.

Economic Organization

1. _____ consumption occurs when most of the food and goods is consumed by the producer and his/her immediate family.

2. _____ is the mode of exchange involving the equal giving and receiving of goods and services between persons of specific statuses.

3. _____ involves the moving of goods and services toward an allocative center.

4. _____ is the direct exchange of one product or service for another through bargaining and without a standard medium of exchange.

5. _____ was used as a medium of exchange by the Iroquois and other Native American societies.

6. The _____ of the Trobriand Islanders is an interisland exchange system.

Social Organization

1. The set of behavior patterns associated with a particular status is the individual's _____.

2. _____ help individuals handle the stress that often accompanies changes in status, known as life crises.

3. The _____ system of India is probably the most rigid of all systems of social stratification.

4. _____ is the rule that encourages people to marry outside a certain group to which they belong.

5. A _____ is the marriage of a woman to her husband's brother upon her husband's death.

6. _____ is the prevailing form of marriage even where polygamy is permitted.

7. The _____ is composed of one set of parents and their children.

8. The residence rule in which the couple resides with or near the bride's family is called _____.

9. The _____ is a unilineal kinship group that traces descent from a known ancestor.

10. A _____ is a unilineal kinship group that traces descent from a remote, often mythical, ancestor.

Political Organization

1. If an association includes all those of a certain age range, it is called _____.

2. Until modern times, most associations were _____ (male/female) oriented.

3. The simplest form of political organization is the small, territorially based group known as the _____.

4. When a government in the form of centralized authority directs and organizes social policy on behalf of the whole society, the association has become a _____.

5. The three basic characteristics of law are: the legitimate use of coercion, predictability and _____.

Ideology, The Arts and Language

1. _____ is the system of beliefs that explains a people's existence and their relation to others, the world and the universe.

2. If the system described above includes a belief in supernatural beings it is called _____.

3. The belief in supernatural beings itself is called _____.

4. _____ is an impersonal force or energy believed to reside in certain people, places or things.

5. The way individuals in a society perceive their total environment is known as their _____.

6. _____ are the primitive accounts of the origin and history of a people and their deities, ancestors and heroes.

7. _____ is the prohibition of something from use, approach or mention because of its sacred nature.

8. A _____ is a religious specialist whose power comes directly from super-natural forces.

9. When magic is used for evil purposes, it is called _____.

10. The conscious production or arrangement of sounds, colors, form or movements in a manner that affects the sense of beauty is called _____.

11. Linguistic anthropologists are concerned with the ways in which _____, culture and society are related.

Post-Test

Circle the correct answer.

1. The integrated total of learned behavior shared by members of a society is its _____.

    A. Environment   B. Culture   C. Status

2. The equal giving and receiving of goods and services between persons of specific statuses is _____.

    A. Reciprocity   B. Redistribution   C. Market Exchange

3. A _____ is a complex, extremely rigid system of social stratification.

    A. Class   B. Caste   C. Status

4. _____ rule encourages people to marry outside a certain social group to which they belong.

    A. Affinal   B. Endogamous   C. Exogamous

5. Marriage of a woman to more than one man at one time is _____.

    A. Polyandry   B. Polygyny   C. Monogamy

6. Another term for conjugal-natal family is _____.

    A. Extended family   B. Nuclear family   C. Joint family

7. Residence rule in which the couple settles with or near the husband's mother's brother is __.

    A. Ambilocal   B. Avunculocal   C. Uxorilocal

8. A _____ reckons descent from both parents.

    A. Kindred   B. Lineage   C. Clan

9. _____ describes kinship based upon marriage.

    A. Consanguineous   B. Cognatic   C. Affinal

10. A belief in supernatural beings is called _____.

    A. Animism   B. Ideology   C. Sorcery

Crossword Puzzle

Across

5. Initials of 46 down.
6. A universal status.
8. A description of a culture.
11. A brother or sister.
13. To adjust to one's environment.
15. A Plains Indian, for example.
17. A well-known physical anthropologist.
18. A social stratus of people sharing similar wealth, power and prestige.
19. What 15 across does (infinitive).
21. Residence rule requiring marriage within a group.
22. The primary unit of human culture.
23. Its invention eased land transportation.
26. Matrilineal descent is traced through this person.
28. Form of containers popular with nomadic peoples.
30. Set of behaviors associated with a status.
32. Religious leader who gets power from supernatural source.
34. Whom a couple settles with in avunculocal rule.
36. Linking of more than two clans in a society.
37. A masculine possessive pronoun.
38. The belief in spirit beings.
40. A social norm which, if violated, evokes sanctions upon the wrongdoer.
41. Number of wives in a polyandrous marriage.
42. A system that classifies statuses and roles of relatives.
45. Prohibition of an act for fear of supernatural punishment.
47. In kinship analysis, the hypothetical point of reference.
48. American anthropologist who wrote *Coming of Age in Samoa*.
50. To search for food.
52. Residence rule without regard to parents' residence.
53. Total.

Down

1. Concern of linguists.
2. Directs and organizes social policy on behalf of entire society.
3. A population acting in accordance with a distinctive culture.
4. A ceremonial act.
5. An important discovery.
7. Theory of adaptive modification.
9. A relative position of degree of value in society.
10. A marriage involving multiple spouses.
12. A stratified, endogamous group to which membership is ascribed by birth.
14. Type of region where irrigation is important.
16. Ages of man named by materials used for these.
18. Learned behavior characteristic of a society.
20. Belief that a magical force resides in certain people, places or things.
24. Tool important in incipient agriculture.
25. Social position of an individual in reference to other members of the society.
27. Period of time.
28. A small, territorially-based social group.
29. Same as 42 across.
31. Marriage to deceased husband's brother.
32. Use of magic for evil purposes.
33. Social institution regulating relations of a mated pair.
35. Unilineal descent group traced from unknown or mythical ancestor.
36. Its invention led to intensive agriculture.
39. Marriage of one man to one woman.
43. Genus which includes man.
44. Has no fixed home.
46. German-born American anthropologist.
49. A universal status.
51. Same as 24 down.

Answers to Tests, Quizzes and Crossword Puzzle

Pre-Test

1. B	6. A
2. A	7. B
3. B	8. A
4. C	9. C
5. B	10. C

Quiz After Page 9

1. Culture
2. Archaeology
3. Diffusion
4. Physical
5. Linguistics
6. Franz Boas

Quiz After Page 15

1. *Homo sapiens sapiens*
2. Charles Darwin
3. Natural selection
4. Primates
5. Hominid
6. Paleolithic
7. Closed

Quiz After Page 27

1. Hunting and gathering
2. Intensive foraging
3. Incipient agriculture (Horticulture)
4. Pastoralism
5. Plow
6. Civilization
7. Agriculture
8. False
9. Wheel
10. Basketry

Quiz After Page 31

1. Primary
2. Reciprocity
3. Redistribution
4. Barter
5. Wampum
6. Kula ring

Quiz After Page 48

1. Role
2. Transition rites
3. Caste
4. Exogamy
5. Levirate
6. Monogamy
7. Nuclear family (Conjugal-natal family)
8. Uxorilocal (Matrilocal)
9. Lineage
10. Clan

Quiz After Page 52

1. Age set, age class or age grade
2. Male
3. Band
4. State
5. Privileged party to apply the coercion

Quiz After Page 63

1. Ideology
2. Religion
3. Animism
4. Mana
5. World View
6. Myths
7. Taboo
8. Shaman
9. Sorcery
10. Art
11. Language

Post-Test

1. B	6. B
2. A	7. B
3. B	8. A
4. C	9. C
5. A	10. A

Answers to Crossword Puzzle:

Glossary

acculturation—process by which the culture of one society is modified to conform to the culture of a dominant society.

adaptation—adjustment made by a living being in order to survive in a particular environment.

affinal—related by marriage.

ambilocal (bilocal)—residence rule in which couple establishes residence near or with either set of parents.

animism—belief in existence of spiritual beings.

archaeology—subfield of anthropology that studies material remains of human workmanship.

artifact—object made by humans.

avunculocal—practice of setting up residency with or near husband's mother's brother.

band—simple, territorially based social group.

caste—stratified, endogamous group of people.

chiefdom—transitional form of political organization between tribal society and the state.

class—social stratum in a non-ranked system, composed of persons sharing similar wealth and prestige.

cognatic kin—relatives on both sides of family.

consanguineous—related by blood.

culture—integrated sum total of learned behavior characteristic of a society.

diffusion—process by which culture elements spread to other societies.

enculturation—process by which the individual learns the patterns of the culture of the society of which he or she is a member.

endogamy—rule that requires marriage within a group.

ethnography—description of a culture.

ethnology—analysis, interpretation and comparison of cultures and societies.

family, conjugal-natal—kinship group to which an individual belongs. Also called nuclear family.

hominid—having human characteristics.

incest taboo—prohibition of sexual relations between closely related persons.

lineage—unilineal kinship group that traces descent from a known common ancestor.

mana—magical force or energy believed to reside in various objects, places and persons.

matrilineal—pertaining to descent through mother.

monogamy—marriage of one man to one woman.

neolocal—practice of establishing a household without regard to that of parents.

patrilineal—pertaining to descent through father.

polyandry—marriage of woman to more than one man.

polygamy—marriage involving multiple spouses.

polygyny—marriage of man to more than one woman.

primitive—pertaining to a culture without a written language.

role—customary complex of behavior associated with a particular status.

society—spatially identifiable human population that acts in accordance with a distinctive culture.

sorcery—use of supernatural power (magic) for evil purposes.

species—population of organisms, members of which are genetically related and cannot breed with other species.

status—social position of an individual with reference to other members of the society.

taboo—prohibition excluding something from use, approach or mention because of its sacred and inviolable nature. Violation is punishable by supernatural powers.

unilineal—pertaining to descent through one parent only.

uxorilocal(matrilocal)—practice of a couple residing with or near wife's family.

virilocal (patrilocal)—practice of a couple residing with or near husband's family.

world view—way in which members of a society perceive their total environment.

Answers and Background Information to Activities

What Is Anthropology? (pages 5-8)

1. In order to assure validity, statements made by informants must be compared with those made by other informants and/or other sources of information. A large enough number of people must be interviewed in order to take into account the variation that may occur within the groups. Informants should be of both sexes and of as many different ages, social positions and locales as possible. If possible, the anthropologist should learn the language of the people he or she is studying; if not, an interpreter is necessary. The anthropologist must stay "in the field" for a long enough time to be sure that what he or she sees is typical.

2. Human beings share certain biologically determined needs for survival: food, shelter, economic and social cooperation and reduction of sexual tension.

4. Natural selection is the principle that individuals possessing characteristics advantageous for survival in a specific environment constitute an increasing proportion of their species in that environment with each succeeding generation. From time to time mutations, or heritable changes in the genes or chromosomes of an organism, occur. Sometimes the mutations are so extreme that the individual never gets born. If a mutation makes an animal weaker, it would be more likely to die at an earlier age. On the other hand, if a mutation happens to make an animal stronger—or, as in the case of human beings, smarter—that animal would have a better chance of living longer. It would probably have more children as well; many of the children would inherit the new trait. It would make them stronger (or smarter, etc.) and they, too, would live longer and have more children. In time the mutation would become characteristic of the species. In the case of humans, their increased brain power enabled them to make and use tools and to outsmart their enemies in the competition for food.

5.

Morgan's Description of Successive Eras		
Stages	**Trait**	**Representative Societies**
1. Lower Savagery	Transitional from ape to human	No known surviving populations
2. Middle Savagery	Development of Speech Control of Fire, and Hunting & Fishing Subsistence	Australian aborigines
3. Upper Savagery	Invention and use of bow and arrow	Polynesians
4. Lower Barbarism	Invention and use of pottery	Iroquois
5. Middle Barbarism	Domestication of plants and animals, irrigation and adobe-brick architecture (New World)	Pueblos, Incas and Aztecs
6. Upper Barbarism	Use of iron tools and weapons	Homeric Greece
7. Civilization A. Ancient B. Modern	Invention of writing	Ancient Egypt

6. Animism is the belief in spirit beings. Tylor concluded that this belief is the principal element of all religion and that it is the result of natural human experiences such as death, sleep, dreams and hallucinations. Dreams, for example are only illusions; however, the experiences seem real to the person who dreams them. This is in spite of the fact that the dreamer knows that his or her body has not left its resting place. This phenomenon led to the idea that there are two parts to an individual: the body and the soul. The concept of a soul is the basic principle of animism. Tylor used this theory to develop a classification of religions. Tylor's theory has been criticized for its sole concentration on the psychological interpretation; however, this theory and his classification were very convincing. Although speculative and unverifiable, many still believe his theory to be highly probable.

7. Ruth Benedict's (1883-1960) fieldwork among Native Americans of the southwestern part of the United States resulted in her study of Zuñi mythology. Her most famous work was *Patterns of Culture* (1934). In it she described how forms of behavior are integrated into patterns or configurations. She believed in cultural relativism, which means that a trait or pattern must be judged in the context of the culture in which it occurs. Her *Chrysanthemum and the Sword* (1946), based upon the study of Japanese culture, helped ease United States-Japanese tensions after World War II.

Alfred L. Kroeber's (1876-1960) efforts covered all areas of anthropology, but his contributions to Native American ethnology, the archaeology of New Mexico, Mexico and Peru and the study of linguistics, folklore, kinship and social structure were especially important. Although he published many important works, his most influential was probably *Anthropology* (1923; revised edition, 1948), one of the first general textbooks on the subject.

Margaret Mead (1901-1978) is best known for her studies of nonliterate people of Oceania and for her analyses of contemporary social problems. Mead's primary interest was in psychology and culture. Her first and probably best-known work was *Coming of Age in Samoa*.

Edward Sapir (1884-1939) is best known for his contributions to the study of Native American languages. He was also one of the founders of ethnolinguistics, which studies the relationship of culture to language. His most influential work was *Language* (1921).

8. Organized crime is an aspect of culture that has a positive function for the criminals who benefit from it. It has a negative function for the rest of society.

Human Evolution (pages 9-12)

1. Primates have grasping hands with flat nails rather than claws; they have acute, stereoscopic vision because their eyes are placed at the front of the head rather than at the sides (higher primates also see in color); and they are able to hold the body in a vertical position during feeding and/or moving.

3. When hands were no longer needed for locomotion, they became available to manufacture and use tools. Because their mouths were no longer needed to get and carry food, they could adapt to articulate more complicated sounds.

4.

Gibbon   Chimpanzee (Ape)

Homo (Human)

5. Just as studies of two human societies would show cultural differences, so might the studies of two different chimpanzee troops show cultural differences.

6. Olduvai Gorge is located in the eastern Serengeti Plains of northern Tanzania. It is a steep-sided ravine about 30 miles (48 kilometers) long and 295 feet (90 meters) deep. A large number of fossil bones have been found there. Seven main stratigraphic layers have been designated. The oldest, Bed I, is about 1,700,000 to 2,100,000 years old. Numerous fossil fauna, including hominids, have been discovered there. It also contains the longest known archaeological record of stone tool industries.

7. "Extant" should be circled.

8. Even in warm climates nights get cool, especially at higher altitudes. The fire provided warmth. As the species moved north, the extra warmth would have become even more important. Also, fire provided light, enabling them to extend their day. This would have given them more chance to interact with each other and a focal point, the campfire, around which they could gather. Already a social animal, this would have encouraged them to become even more social. Fire might also have been accidental or out of curiosity rather than need.

9. Farmers plowing fields, construction workers clearing the ground for buildings or roads and soldiers are among those who might unearth artifacts by chance.

10. The Mousterian complex (which lasted from about 100,000 to 35,000 years ago) continued the technological trend that had been developing during the Lower and Middle Paleolithic Ages. It still had small hand axes, but flake tools became most important. Also found were round limestone balls, probably used to hurl at animals. Wooden spears were used to hunt mammoth and other large game.

11.

	Lower Pleistocene			Middle Pleistocene					Upper Pleistocene	
	2,000,000 to 5,000,000 B.C.	900,000	800,000	700,000	600,000	500,000	400,000	300,000	200,000	100,000
Homo sapiens						*Homo sapiens steinheimensis (palestinus)*			*Homo sapiens neandertalensis*	*Homo sapiens sapiens*
Homo erectus				*Homo erectus mauritanicus*	*Homo erectus erectus*	*Homo erectus pekinensis*			*Homo erectus soloensis*	*Homo erectus rhodesianensis*
Australopithecus		*Australopithecus africanus*	*Australopithecus robustus*	*Australopithecus boisei*						

12. It was easier for the Europeans to accept Cro-Magnons as their ancestors, for they appeared more like northwestern Europeans than other fossil groups. They were large brained, high domed and upright. What's more, they produced an excellent art.

13. Louis Seymour Bazett (L.S.B.) Leakey began his search for prehistoric life in East Africa in 1924. His work at Olduvai Gorge in Tanzania, which became the site of his most famous discoveries, started in 1831. The fossil discoveries made by L.S.B. and his wife Mary proved that humans were much older than scientists had previously believed. Their work also showed that human evolution had been centered in Africa rather than in Asia as the work of earlier anthropologists had suggested. Although Leakey differed from others as to the classification of his finds, the value of his contributions have been recognized by most, if not all.

The Ages of Man (page 13)
1. We live in the Atomic or Nuclear Age.

2. There was overlapping, for the ages of civilization did not begin at the same time in all places.

Human Variation (pages 14-15)

1. Members of a species are capable of interbreeding and incapable of breeding with members of other species. Within a species there may be populations in which certain genes occur in greater or lesser frequencies than in other populations of the species; however, members of these populations are still capable of breeding with other members of the species.

3. People living in warm, humid regions generally have greater pigmentation than those living near the poles. The dark skin and hair color comes from a greater amount of melanin. One hypothesis for this variation is based upon our need for Vitamin D, which helps our bodies absorb calcium. A deficiency in Vitamin D leads to soft bones and rickets. The primary source of Vitamin D (before vitamins were added to enrich foods) was the absorption of ultraviolet rays from the sun. These rays stimulate the body to produce its own Vitamin D. Too much Vitamin D, however, is also dangerous. It can cause calcification, or hardening of the soft tissues. In hot, nonfrostal areas, dark skin would screen out some of the rays to prevent the body from making too much Vitamin D. In cooler, cloud-covered areas, light skin would allow greater amounts of sunlight to penetrate and, therefore, greater amounts of Vitamin D to be produced. Those with the proper amounts of melanin to suit their environments would have survived at greater rates to pass on the same trait to their offspring.

4. The Eskimo body build is a near perfect adaptation to life in the frigid areas of the north. The smaller the skin area in relation to a person's total body volume, the less skin to be cooled by the freezing conditions; therefore, the short, stocky bodies of the Eskimos are helpful in conserving heat. The heavy layers of subcutaneous fat not only help hold in the body heat, but also help pull them through the periods of time when food supplies are scarce. Their heavy, fatty double eyelids protect their eyes from the frigid air and from the blinding reflections of the snow. Their flat brows and pudgy cheeks protect their delicate sinuses. The fact that their noses are small and flat provides less of an opportunity for them to become frostbitten.

Culture and Society (page 16)

3. A society is composed of people. A culture comprises the behavior, rules, beliefs and products of those people. A person belongs to a society, but he or she does not belong to a culture.

4. In their book *Social Life, Structure, and Function* J.W. Bennett and M.M. Tumin identify the prerequisites of a culture: to maintain the biological functioning of the group members; to reproduce new members; to produce and distribute necessary goods and services; to maintain order (within the group and between the group and others); and to define the "meaning of life" and maintain the motivation to survive and engage in activities necessary for survival.

Subsistence Techniques (pages 17-20)

1. Gathering involves the use of the resources of the environment without the means to improve or increase supplies. It involves hunting and fishing as well as the collection of wild plants. Production, on the other hand, utilizes techniques such as farming and/or domestication of animals in order to improve and increase food supplies.

2. If less energy is needed to produce food, then more is available for other social uses. Most likely, this would result in increasingly complex social institutions and organization. More advanced food-getting techniques make it possible to stay in one place and to acquire more goods. More goods lead to trade, social status based upon wealth, etc.

3. They usually have small populations. (Exceptions have been found in societies off the Pacific Coast and Great Plains where there is an abundance of fish, game, berries, nuts, etc.) Their social organization is usually based upon kinship. Recent and contemporary food-gathering societies are usually isolated and without much contact with other societies to influence change.

5. The whalers were extremely skilled; nevertheless, whale hunting involved an enormous amount of danger. They turned to magic and ritual to reinforce their skills and to appeal to the whale spirit for help. Like many peoples whose subsistence is dependent upon hunting, these whalers believed in the spirit nature of their prey—in this case the whale. Also, because the welfare of the society was so dependent upon the hunt, the rituals of the cult served to honor the best hunters and to bestow leadership status upon them.

6. The Shoshone were in constant fear of starvation. Over 100 kinds of seeds, berries and nuts were eaten by them. Sunflower seeds and pine nuts were especially important in their diet. Insects, such as grasshoppers, were considered a real treat. Grasshopper drives were organized in which a large pit about 30' to 40' in diameter and about 3' to 4' deep was dug. The people circled the pit and drove the insects into it with brush beaters. The grasshoppers were then roasted. Ants, also considered a delicacy, were even more prized. While the ants were still in the larval stage, the women would scoop up the nest and gather the ants in their special baskets. After toasting them, they were ground, rolled out and made into a paste. The Shoshone rounded out their diets by communal hunting of rabbits and sometimes antelopes. Pitfalls were set up to catch small rodents. Only the most energetic hunters went after a deer, mountain goat or mountain sheep; they would have to chase them for two days until the prey was so tired that the hunter could get close enough to shoot. The few things the Shoshone would not eat included wolves, coyotes and their cousins the dogs. Coyote was a supernatural culture hero, believed to be the younger brother of Wolf. Wolf himself was thought by some groups to be the Supreme Deity.

7. Although horticulture is often associated with the use of a hoe, an even more important tool was the dibble, a pointed instrument used to make holes in the soil; it was also called a digging stick. Hoes and spades were also used to turn over the soil; however, unless the people learned to use metal, hoes and spades (made of wood, shell or bone) could only be used for light cultivation.

8. First the trees were killed by cutting a ring through the bark. The dead trees were either left standing or burned away. Then the seeds were planted around the dead stumps. After a few years, when the nutrients were depleted, the gardeners moved to other sites.

9. Because horticultural societies had more secure and more abundant food supplies than the hunter-gatherers, they were able to stay in one place for longer periods of time. They were also able to feed more people and their populations grew larger. The more they learned, the more their food supplies increased, and the larger their populations became. As the populations spread out to other areas, the people had to adapt to those new environments and to the new plant and animal life in them. In many areas, the people began to produce and preserve a surplus. This enabled them to engage in other activities not directly related to the quest for food. Some specialized in the making of tools or other artifacts. Others became warriors or religious and political leaders. There was a growing reliance on redistribution of wealth (a chief, etc., received goods and services and distributed the surpluses) and trade. In time wealth accumulation became possible. This in turn led to social stratification and a shift from the family as the basis of authority to a political system.

10. Practical uses of domesticated animals include a source of food (meat, eggs, blood); use of their hides for clothing and shelter; use of their wool for weaving or felting; milking and dairying; transport of goods; riding; means of exchange and reciprocity; and their dung, as fuel or fertilizer.

11. The animals would be protected from predators. The herdsman would do his best to provide water, food and shelter. The animals might be cared for when ill, and if not, at least isolated from those who are ill to prevent the spread of the disease. The herdsman might help the animals with difficult births and care for the young when necessary.

12. Large-scale irrigation is a complex system and requires a higher level of organization. The person who has control of the water has control of a scarce—and vital—commodity! The ruler and his support group have the power to provide or deny access to drainage channels and irrigation works upon which

the populations are dependent. The tremendous task of administering the huge waterworks not only creates a need for centralized government, it also provides that government with its source of power. In many parts of the ancient world, the chiefdoms were destroyed or assimilated by the emergent states.

Technological Adaptations (pages 22-27)
Shelter (page 22)

2. How to build an igloo: 1) Start with snow that is neither too soft nor too loose. Do not use drift snow. 2) Use a probe made of reindeer horn, bone or wood to be sure that the snow is of the proper consistency and that there is enough of it. 3) Use your snow knife with its slightly curved blade to strike vertically into the snow. 4) One worker will cut out the blocks and the other will place them. 5) Cut out a block two feet wide, three feet long and one foot thick. 6) Shake it gently to loosen the base. 7) Lift it out. 8) Carve out the block next to it in a similar fashion. 9) Continue to cut the blocks, leaving a circular depression that will be the base of the igloo. 10) Set each row of blocks upon the lower one so that each is slightly inward until a dome is formed. 11) Leave a small hole at the top. 12) Cut out a door to let yourself out. 13) Cut the last brick to size and fit it to the hole on the top. 14) Fill in holes with loose snow. 15) Throw loose snow around the outside base to help keep out the cold. 16) Build a tunnel leading out and down from the entrance; it should be lower than the floor to keep out the cold air. 17) Cut out a small section of the wall above the entrance. Put in a piece of clear ice which has been previously cut from the river or lake. 18) You may wish to cut out a small hole in the roof for ventilation. 19) Place skins on the raised platform inside the igloo on which to eat, work and sleep.

3. The Native Americans of the Plains were buffalo hunters and, therefore, needed movable dwellings. The skin tipis were comfortable and well built. They offered a great deal of resistance to the wind, heat and cold of the changeable Plains environment. They were easy to dismantle and, as they had dogs and horses with which to set up a travois, easily transportable during their many moves. Once at their new site, the tipis were easily and quickly set up again.

4.

5. The great emphasis upon cooperation among families and clans was reflected in the multistoried, compact communal dwellings in which members were forced to live in close intimacy. Just as the great building was designed to keep out the outer world, so did the Pueblo culture seek to keep out outsiders.

Clothing and Ornaments (page 23)
3. Two basic statuses represented by hairstyles are sex and age.

4. In Polynesia tatooing is associated with high social status. In fact, the higher the social status, the larger the area of the body which is covered with tatoos. In America, it is among the lower ranks that tatooing symbolizes strength and masculinity. People of higher status usually look down upon it.

Transport (page 24)
1. Some forms of land transport are: the dog or horse travois; sleds, sledges and toboggans; pack animals; and early wheeled vehicles such as two-wheeled carts. Water transport includes simple logs and inflated skins to support swimmers; reed rafts; log rafts; coracles (small, rounded boats covered with skin); dugout canoes; birch bark canoes; kayaks; and outriggers.

3. The wheel greatly minimizes friction; therefore, the same amount of force is capable of moving a much greater weight. All other significant machines are based upon the principle of the wheel.

4. Boats and other innovations made it possible for people to come into contact with groups living at a greater distance. Ocean travel resulted in radical changes. Europeans were introduced to the ideas, customs and other elements of distant cultures. People who had previously lived in isolation would find it more and more difficult to maintain their old ways.

Tools and Handicrafts (pages 25-27)
1. Materials often used include: shells, wood, bones, leaves, dried gourds, stones, plant fibers and worked animal skins.

2. The other materials—bark, leaves, hide, shell, etc.—would have disintegrated; therefore, there is no direct evidence.

5. Pomo baskets are judged by many to be the finest ever made. They have many practical functions including storage, transportation and cooking baskets. Many of their baskets are so tightly woven that they are watertight even without the use of pitch. They can even be used for cooking by the hot-stone method. (Water was heated by dropping in hot stones with a hinged stick.) Some of their huge storage baskets are large enough to hold several bushels; these are often made with course materials and are not usually decorated. On the other hand, a few of their baskets only have a decorative function, such as those ¼'' in diameter. Of course, many are both useful and beautifully decorated either by weaving in geometric designs or by utilizing colored feathers in the weft.

6. A.

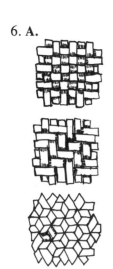

B.

C.

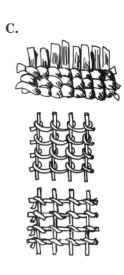

Weaving (A): The most widespread form of weaving is called twilling, in which the warp (fibers that run lengthwise) and weft (horizontal fibers) are of equal thickness and pliability. Common materials for twilling are split cane or bamboo, grass and rice straw. The strands of the warp are set in parallel rows. The weft fibers are passed over and under those of the warp. The result is a checkerboard effect. (Variations in the pattern are easily made.)

Coiling (B): Coiling is accomplished by building up a continuous foundation made of a single rod or a bundle of fibers or splints (or 2 to 3 bundles or rods which have been bound together). The element is coiled spirally, starting in the center of the bottom of the container. Each successive coil is sewn with the use of an awl or needle to the previous one by a sewing element, or weft. Designs are made by using different colored strands of the weft.

Twining (C): In twining the warp may be either rigid or pliable, but the weft must be pliable. Twine is the most common weft element. Each weft element is wrapped in, out and around the warp fibers, which have been set in parallel rows. Sometimes the 2 warp elements are set on each other at right angles; the twine is used to intertwine them.

7.

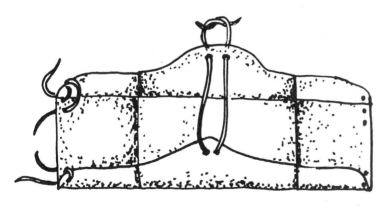

85

8. Pottery is too fragile and too cumbersome to be used extensively by nomadic peoples.

9. Even in ancient times people tended to throw away their broken pottery and to replace it with the more recent style. That makes it valuable to the archaeologist for dating purposes. Also, because the pottery was easy to make and of little value, it was seldom carried away as booty; therefore, it is usually representative of the site at which it was found.

10. The four phases of working metal include: 1) mining, or extracting the ore-bearing materials from the earth; 2) smelting, or the process of extracting metal from ore or sand by intense heating; 3) alloying, or mixing of metals to produce a more useful material; and 4) forging or casting, methods by which to shape the metal into useful artifacts.

ECONOMIC ORGANIZATION (pages 28-31)

2. Most societies are territorially based. Their subsistence is drawn from the soil either directly or indirectly. Of course, it is the food itself that is of primary importance to an individual.

3. Primogeniture is the right of the eldest child (usually son) to inherit the entire estate of one or both parents in order to prevent inefficient dispersal. He then supports the other members of the family; they work for him. Primogeniture does not apply only to landed property, but also to the succession to chiefdom and office. In some cases it encourages the younger siblings to go out and gain new lands and to found new lineages.

4. Pastoralists usually move within a certain territory as a group; however, if the resources have been depleted, they must move to new pastures and watering places, at least until the supplies in their territory have been replenished. Conflicts frequently occur when farmers do not feel the land belongs to the pastoralists because they are not permanently settled there. As the pastoral people are more mobile, they are often able to raid, dominate or conquer larger groups of settled farmers. The conflict between the cattlemen and the farmers during the expansion of the United States frontier is a prime example.

6. Wampum, short for wampumpeag, were the small cylindrical beads used by Native Americans. They were in use before any European contact was made. The beads were made from clam and whelk shells by Algonquian Indian groups that lived along the New England and Mid-Atlantic coasts. They were greatly valued by the Iroquois, who wove the beads into belts and strung them on leather thongs. Wampum was used not only as jewelry, but also to record laws and ceremonies and to confirm treaties and other agreements. A sachem, or chief, of the Onandaga Nation was the Keeper of the Wampum and its official interpreter. Wampum beads were always valued by the Native Americans and were often traded. Most of the wampum beads were white. Some beads were made from the dark purple lining of the quahog shell. Because these were rarer and more difficult to make, they were more highly valued. With one exception*, the wampum had no fixed value until the arrival of the Europeans. The Europeans, finding them useful as change, valued them at a half-penny per white bead.

*A murderer had to pay six strings to the victim's family if they agreed to accept payment rather than have him killed.

7. Reciprocity, Redistribution and Market Exchange should be filled in the blanks.

8. The bond between trading partners is solidified by the highly ritualized exchange of gifts. The system provides an atmosphere of friendship, confidence, appreciation and cooperation in which to deal. Each partner feels as if he is benefiting from the relationship while maintaining his self-esteem. Despite the elaborate rituals, the main function of the Kula was the distribution of goods. Eventually, the Trobrianders succeeded in distributing their locally grown and produced goods throughout the islands.

Social Organization (pages 32-49)

2. This need to belong to a group is a result of long periods of human dependency in infancy and early childhood. During this period the human being must learn the behaviors necessary to survive. Because most human behavior is learned rather than instinctive, the young human must be protected by a group, usually the family. Humans continue to acquire their patterns of behavior, techniques, attitudes, beliefs and values from the family and other groups to which they belong.

3. Statuses which are attained through competitive mastery of behaviors are said to be achieved. Examples are lawyer, dancer, author and artist. These statuses can only be attained by **first** mastering the roles. Statuses which are attained because of age, sex or kinship are said to be ascribed. It is not necessary to master the roles before attaining these statuses. Unlike achieved statuses, ascribed statuses precede mastery of the roles associated with them.

5. In a stable society the young can learn from their elders. Their knowledge is a source of prestige. In a rapidly changing society, what the elderly learned may no longer be valid; therefore, it is no longer a source of prestige.

7. To some extent names imply a number of statuses. Many peoples give their children names associated with good deeds or good luck in the hope that the name will bring the same to the child. Names sometimes are associated with certain social or ethnic groups. Nicknames are often given that are associated with certain ascribed statuses, such as age, or achieved statuses, such as boxer. For example, a boy officially named William Michael Smith might be called Billy as a child. If he grows up to be a boxer, perhaps his nickname will be Rocky. If he grows up to be a business executive, it might be W.M. If he grows up to be a teacher, his students will call him Mr. Smith, and so on.

Potlatch (pages 35-36)

1. Coppers, which are flat sheets of copper in the shape of shields, were prized as symbols of wealth. The Native American tribes of the North Pacific Coast obtained the metal from tribes of the interior. They beat the copper into its characteristic shape. They were about 3/16'' thick and up to 3 feet high, although most were smaller. The lower half was rectangular and the upper half somewhat like a rounded trapezoid. Ridges divided the top from the bottom. Coppers were decorated by engraving or painting. The more they were traded, the more their value increased.

2. Some possible tribes are: the Yurok and the Karok of California; the Chinook of the Columbia River; the Quinault, the Quileute and the Makah of Vancouver Island; the Bella Coola of British Columbia; the Haida of Queen Charlotte's Island; the Tsimshian of British Columbia; the Tlingit of southern Alaska; and the Chilkat of northern Alaska.

Caste (pages 37-38)

1. In traditional Japanese society the Eta were at the lowest level of the social system. They had to stay in their own districts and were forbidden to marry out of their group. The mere presence of the Eta was deemed polluting to any member of a higher status. Because they were mostly butchers, tanners and leather workers, it is likely that their low status originated because their occupations involved the taking of animal life. When Buddhism, with its reverence for life, spread in the 7th century, the already low status probably sank even lower. In 1868 laws were established to remove restrictions on the Eta, but prejudice remained.

Mating and Marriage (pages 39-40)

1. Mendel and his followers showed that hereditary materials are carried in our genes and that each parent contributes one gene to the offspring. Inbreeding increases the chances of passing on destructive genes that may have been inherited by a brother and sister from their parent or parents.

2. These fighting, pastoral people benefited from the uniting of their herds and manpower to combat the assaults of other local lineages in competition with them.

3. Jacob went to the house of Laban, his mother's brother. Jacob offered to work for Laban for seven years in exchange for the promise of Laban's daughter Rachel as his wife. Laban agreed, but when the seven years were over, he gave Jacob his older daughter, Leah, instead. He said that if Jacob wanted Rachel, he would have to work an additional seven years. Jacob worked seven more years and married Rachel, too.

4. Monogamy is the marriage of one man to one woman. Polygyny is the marriage of one man to more than one woman at a time. Polyandry, which is rare, is the marriage of one woman to more than one man at a time.

In most societies the male and female populations are usually about the same size. (An exception might be during times of war.) If polygyny were the most common form, a large segment of the population would remain unmarried. This would probably lead to stressful conditions.

The Nuclear Family (pages 41-42)

2. Congugal : Family of Procreation::Natal : Family of Orientation

3.

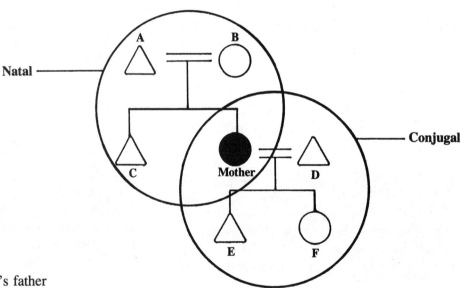

A: Mother's father
B: Mother's mother
C: Mother's brother
D: Mother's husband
E. Mother's son
F. Mother's daughter

NOTE: Charts will vary according to the number of siblings and offspring.

4.

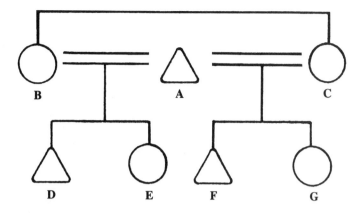

A: Man
B: Sister to whom man is married
C: Sister to whom man is married
D: Male offspring of man by wife B
E: Female offspring of man by wife B
F: Male offspring of man by wife C
G: Female offspring of man by wife C

5. The man's wealth and prestige would increase and, therefore, so would the prestige and wealth of his wife and her children. The wives share the labor and help each other during child-bearing and child-rearing. They might also provide each other with companionship.

Residence Patterns (page 43)
1. When the couple resides at a distance from relatives, they may find themselves amongst strangers. They must provide for the needs of their spouse without the help of their kin, thereby increasing the possibilities of stress. Also, if problems arise in their relationship, there are no relatives to intervene and help them work things out. On the other hand, neolocal patterns of residency promote privacy, provide greater living space, encourage independence and responsibility and reduce conflict and tension between members outside the nuclear family.

2. Societies which depend upon the solidarity of the male group for their subsistence and for the allocation and distribution of goods, such as hunters and pastoralists or advanced farmers, usually prefer the virilocal, or patrilocal, residence rule; this is especially true if the men are depended upon to protect the group from hostile outsiders. Societies which depend upon primitive farming, in which women play a major role in the production, allocation and distribution of goods, usually prefer uxorilocal residence, especially if stable relations with their neighbors exist. In these societies, when technology advances, there is often a change to avunculocal residence, which is male-dominated, but still matrilineally based. Biolocal residence often occurs in societies with an unstable technological base because it allows for the most mobility. There is usually little fixed property in these societies.

3. Even in a society with a patrilocal or virilocal residence rule, the bride would not feel the strain nearly as much if village endogamy were the custom, for her family would still be close by and she could still maintain close relations with her kin.

4. There are reciprocal economic, social and ritual ties. For example, they aid each other in the care and enculturation of the young and the production and distribution of goods. They lend emotional support in times of stress.

Kinship Groups (pages 44-45)

1. The kindred is a personal group. It includes any person to whom an individual can trace a genealogical bond. Membership in a kindred is different for every person. Only a sibling can share the same kindred. It cannot function as a group except in relation to "ego," the term used to designate the hypothetical point of reference in analyzing kinship relations.

3. By tracing descent through only one person, the kinship is more clear-cut. It reduces the number of potential members. It solidifies the relationships among the members of the group and lessons the chance that an individual will become involved in conflicting or incompatible obligations.

Kinship Terms (pages 46-47)

1.

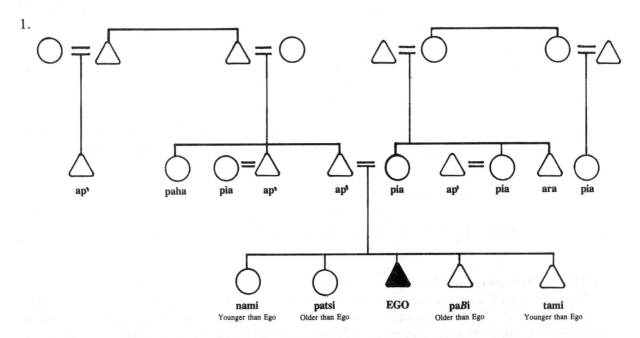

2. Both systems identify a difference in generation levels. Only the Comanches identify a difference in age levels within the same generation. The Anglo-American system distinguishes between lineal relationships (through an ancestor) and collateral, or nondirect, relationships (related through siblings of father or mother or other lineals). The terms of both systems distinguish between the sex of the relatives, but only the Comanche identifies differences in the sex of the speaker or the sex of the person through whom the relationship is established. The Anglo-American system strongly emphasizes the conjugal-natal family. This reflects the great social significance of close relatives as compared with the larger kindred. Monogamy is reflected in the fact that words like *father, mother, husband* and *wife* can only apply to one person within the kinship system. For the Comanches, the larger kindred is more important; therefore, many individuals are merged.

Associations and Age Groups (pages 48-49)

1. The rituals serve to intensify the youth's awareness of his rights and obligations and to intensify the community's awareness of the boy's new status.

2. Native American tribes with age-graded associations include the Mandan, Hidatsa, Arapaho, Gros Ventre and Blackfoot.

3. In order to take advantage of new job opportunities that become available, many people leave the homogeneous community in which they were raised and migrate to an unfamiliar setting. This results in a breakdown of traditional groupings based upon kinship. The individual (and the individual's nuclear family) often feels isolated and searches for an alternative source of support to replace the support that had been provided by the kinship group. Voluntary associations may offer economic and political protection as well as companionship and entertainment. They also help to enculturate the individual and help him/her adjust to the new cultural setting.

Political Organization (pages 50-52)

1. The functions of government include the definition of behavioral norms; the allocation of force and authority; the settlement of disputes; the organization of public works; the redistribution of goods and the control of markets; and the defense against enemy societies.

2. No person can actually rule alone. All governments include a council in one form or another. Even a king or a chief works with a network of advisers and depends upon the support of others in order to maintain his position. Like any other social relation, the relation between a monarch and his subjects rests upon reciprocity.

3. Regularity is a common characteristic of law and custom.

4. The !Kung authority system is workable only when the tribe remains isolated from technologically advanced societies with highly organized political systems. Their system does not provide an adequate means of organization or unification against outside intruders. Many have been killed or assimilated by technologically superior peoples who took over their land.

5. The man would have married the wife and adopted their children. When the dead man's son came of age, he would slay him in revenge for the murder of his father. His death would then have to be avenged and the feud would continue.

Ideology and Religion (pages 53-58)

2. Most people would believe it was the result of the skill and effort of the fisherman. (Although the fisherman might be reluctant to change spears!)

3. Some common objects believed to have mana are four-leaf clovers, horseshoes, rabbits' feet, and lucky shirts and other pieces of clothing.

World View (pages 54-55)

2. There are a tremendous number of diverse, cultural backgrounds represented in the recent immigrant origins of the people of the United States. Beliefs range from atheism to extreme piety. There are vast differences in educational, recreational and occupational interests. There are vast environmental differences; nevertheless, if subgroup and individual differences are not considered, there are some generalizations that can be made: in spite of the fact that the American world view is a derivative of the Judeo-Christian-Hellenistic traditions, the conception of the universe is mechanistic rather than mystic; in other words, phenomena are explained by physical or biological causes rather than religious or mystical causes. The basic premise is that the universe is a physical system which operates according to discoverable scientific laws. Although religion is important for social organization, it is not greatly relied upon as the means to achieve goals. To achieve their goals most people instead rely upon scientific research and its technical application. People must work to improve living conditions and action is emphasized; therefore, there is more concern for practical knowledge than abstract knowledge. Individual responsibility is very important as is the idea of egalitarianism.

Mythology (page 56)

1. Kane shaped and formed two heavens: an Upper Heaven for the gods and goddesses and a Lower Heaven for the Earth he was about to create. He threw a huge calabash into the air. The top of the calabash became the curved bowl, sky. Two other pieces became the sun and the moon. The seeds which scattered in the sky became stars. The rest of the calabash became the Earth. It fell back into the sea. Then he and the other great gods—Ku, Lono and Kanaloa—created the animals and plants to live on the Earth. Finally, the gods brought some rich red earth to Kane. He shaped it into man and breathed life into it. Man would be the chief—the ruler of the Earth.

2. Many of the ancient Greeks believed that in the beginning there was only Chaos—a confused, shapeless mass. In that mass, however, existed the seeds of things. Earth, sea and air were all mixed together. Then the mass separated into Heaven and Earth. The ocean and the land separated. The Earth, being heavier, sank. The water buoyed up the Earth.

Ritual (page 57)

1. The ritual actions serve to reinforce the beliefs. In the minds of the believers they are a way to affect and improve their relations with others, with the world, and with the universe. Above all, the actions are believed to improve one's relations to the supernatural beings upon whose belief the ideology is based.

2. The principal function of taboo is to maintain the sense of mystery and extraordinary power of the supernatural forces. It reinforces the concept that the sacred—that which is viewed as supernatural—must be treated in a careful, special manner by showing that attitudes of carelessness and profanity (as if it were ordinary) will be punished by supernatural sanctions. Another function of taboo is to create a feeling of solidarity among the members of a social group who believe in the same supernatural forces. Taboo is also a means of social control. This is especially true in Polynesia where the word *taboo* originated. The high ranking nobles are believed to descend from the gods and, therefore, to possess mana. They and everything they touch are surrounded by taboos meant to protect them.

3. Shamans exist in religious systems that have not developed a church. They derive their power directly from the supernatural forces upon which the religion is based. Some derive it through the ability to perform rites or the possession of the required paraphernalia. Priests, on the other hand, derive their power from the religious organization itself. They work in a structured hierarchy according to a set of traditions. Shamans are individualists and are not held in check by any bureaucratic control. Religion is a tremendous source of power; therefore, those in whom authority is vested are very powerful individuals, whether shamans or priests. For the same reason, power is always vested in an adult, usually a male. Although female shamans are fairly common, priestesses are not, probably because—until recently—the organization of associations tended to be correlated with the male in most societies.

Magic and Sorcery (page 58)

1. Sometimes magic seems to work because of coincidence; the event eventually would have occurred whether or not the magic was performed. When the magic is performed in order to harm someone, it sometimes works because of psychological suggestion. For example, when a person believes himself an object of magic and when he and others in his social group believe the magic to be effective, the victim may become hysterical, sicken and die. At other times, magic seems to work simply because the magician is clever at deceiving his audience.

2. People who believe their dead continue to be important members of the community generally are less fearful of death than those who view it as an end. They merely see it as a new status, which is accompanied by a reunion with loved ones, veneration by future generations, continued or increased authority and new supernatural power.

The Arts (pages 59-60)

1. The varied art forms labeled "primitive" are seldom crude; when they are, it is usually the artist's intent. Their symbolic meanings are usually quite complex. When these art forms were first seen by Europeans, they evaluated them in terms of classical and Judeo-Christian standards and concepts rather than in terms of the culture of which it was a part.

3. Northwest Coast art tends to be utilitarian; the decorative aesthetic element is limited by the object itself. One characteristic is that no blank spaces may be left. Another is that the designs are symmetrical. Also, the decorative elements represent an aspect of animal life. The animals that are used symbolized a mythical or historical event in the social background of the artist. There are standard ways to portray the characteristics of the traits of each animal. For example, a beaver will have a flat, scaly, mud-slapper tail and sharp cutting teeth. A bear is recognized by its teeth and long claws. Sometimes the animal seems to be split and spread out in order to fill in the spaces.

BEAR

BEAVER

4.

5. African statues are usually disproportionate: the head is large in relation to the torso and the legs are short and thick. Mass, or three-dimensional solidity, is an impressive feature; the thickness and round-ness of the figures are emphasized. The plain, highly-polished surface is another characteristic. Mahogany and ironwood, both hardwood, are common materials; they are close-grained and take a beautiful polish.

6. Forms of verbal art include prose narratives, poetry, riddles, proverbs, myths and legends.

Language and Other Ways to Communicate (pages 61-63)

1. Language plays a vital role in abstract, symbolic thinking. It is the principal medium through which we acquire, store and pass on knowledge. Culture is defined as the integrated sum total of the learned behavior patterns, acts, beliefs and other products of human work and thought characteristic of a social group; therefore, it would be very difficult to have culture without language. It is not necessary, however, for people who share a culture to share the same language. Neither is it necessary for all who share a language to share the same culture.

2.
Indo-European Family of Languages

Germanic	Celtic	Baltic	Slavic	*Romance	Greek	Indo-Iranian	Armenian	Albanian
German	Gaelic	Lithuanian	Russian	Spanish	Greek	Persian	Armenian	Albanian
English	Welsh	Lettish	Polish	French		Kurdish		
Dutch		(Latvians)	Czech	Italian		Modern		
Scandinavian			Bulgarian	Portuguese		languages		
			Serbo-Croatian	*From Latin		of India		

3. In a language such as Latin the morphemic structure is so exact that even if you change the order of the words, the meaning is clear. *Feles equum videt, Videt equum feles,* and *Videt feles equum* all make sense. (The cat sees the horse.) No matter what the order, it is clear who is doing the seeing and who is being seen. In English, however, ''The cat sees the horse'' has a different meaning from ''The horse sees the cat'' and ''Sees the dog the cat'' makes no sense at all!

5. The state of the snow is important to the ski culture; therefore, it makes distinctions similar to those of the Eskimos. Its vocabulary is borrowed from the Austrian Tyrol:

Pappschnee: wet, heavy snow
Kornschnee: barley snow that has melted under spring sunshine and frozen at night
Pulverschnee: powder snow
Fernschnee: broad expanse of breakable crust

9. Writing, when applied in conjunction with other important inventions, such as printing, provides the means for long-distance communication, the keeping of accurate records, and the systems of education and research vital to modern world cultures.

Bibliography

Starred books (*) are appropriate for students. The other titles are for mature readers.

Benedict, Ruth. *Patterns of Culture.* New York: New American Library, 1946.

*Benjamin, Nora. *The First Book of Archaeology.* New York: Franklin Watts, 1957.

Boas, Franz. *The Mind of Primitive Man,* 1911.

———. *Race, Language and Culture,* 1940.

Childe, V.G. ''The Urban Revolution,'' *Town Planning Review,* vol. 21, no.1, 1950.

Evans-Pritchard. *The Nuer.* Oxford: Oxford University Press, 1940.

Hammond, Peter B. *An Introduction to Cultural and Social Anthropology,* 2nd edition. New York: Macmillan Publishing Company, 1978.

Hoebel, E. Adamson. ''Comanche and H3klandika Shoshone Relationship Systems.'' *American Anthropologist* 41 (1939): 440-59.

Hoebel E. Adamson and Thomas Weaver. *Anthropology and the Human Experience,* 5th edition. New York: Mc Graw-Hill Book Company, 1979.

Leakey, Richard E. and Roger Lewin. *Origins.* New York: E.P. Dutton, 1977.

Levi-Strauss, C. *The Elementary Structures of Kinship,* trans. by J.H. Bell, J.R. von Sturmer and R. Needham. Boston, 1969

Malinowski, Bronislaw. *A Scientific Theory of Culture, and Other Essays.* 1944

Mead, Margaret. *Anthropologists and What They Do.* New York: Franklin Watts, 1965.

———. *People and Places.* New York: The World Publishing Company, 1959.

Montagu, Ashley. *Man: His First Two Million Years.* . New York: Columbia University Press, 1969.

Pfeiffer, John E. *The Emergence of Society.* New York: McGraw-Hill Book Co., 1977.

Radcliffe-Brown, A.R. *Structure and Function in Primitive Society,* 1952.

Sapir, Edward. *Language.* New York: Harcourt, 1921.

*Stark, Rebecca. *Native American Cultures.* Hawthorne, NJ: Educational Impressions, Inc., 1992.

*Tunis, Edwin. *Indians.* New York: Thomas Y. Crowell, 1979.

*Underhill, Ruth. *First Came the Family.* New York: William Morrow, 1958